The People of the
Scottish Borders,
1650-1800

The People of the
Scottish Borders,
1650-1800

By David Dobson

CLEARFIELD

Copyright © 2012
by David Dobson
All Rights Reserved

Printed for Clearfield Company by
Genealogical Publishing Company
Baltimore, Maryland
2012

ISBN 978-0-8063-5589-4

Made in the United States of America

INTRODUCTION

This book, 'The People of the Scottish Borders, 1650-1800', is designed to identify people who lived in the counties of Berwickshire, Peebles-shire, Roxburghshire and Selkirkshire, a region now known as the Scottish Borders, which lies in south-eastern Scotland mainly along the border with England. The entries are based overwhelmingly on primary sources, generally documentary, which should enable researchers to flesh out their family trees and build on the information found in church records where it exists. The bulk of the references are based on manuscripts located in the National Archives of Scotland in Edinburgh [now part of the National Records of Scotland] and are taken from court records, registers of deeds, registers of sasines, exchequer records, registers of testaments, burgh records, family and estate papers. Other sources include published monumental inscription lists, government records, and miscellaneous books.

This book also contains reference to a number of early emigrants from the Scottish Borders to the Americas, including George Home in Nova Scotia around 1630 and Robert Gilchrist in Barbados in 1649, as well as a number of Quakers and Covenanters who settled in East New Jersey in the 1680s. Other Borderers are known to have migrated to England, the Netherlands, Ireland and Scandinavia, a handful of them are also listed.

From the medieval period right through until the early seventeenth century the border country adjoining England and Scotland was subject to near continuous conflict caused by invading armies and also by raiders who crossed the border to steal goods and to rustle livestock. These raiders were known as the reivers and were generally composed of members of the same extended family, often bearing the same distinctive surname and were based in the same locality. These reivers existed on both sides of the Anglo-Scottish border. The reiver families based in the East March and Mid March of the Scots side of the frontier, the region now known as the Scottish Borders, bore the following surnames – Cranston, Craw, Crozier, Dalgleish, Davidson, Dickson, Elliot, Gilchrist, Hume, Kerr, Oliver, Pringle, Redpath, Robson, Rutherford, Scott, Tait, Trotter, Turnbull, and Young, all of whom appear in this book. To the west, on the Scots side of the border in what is now Dumfries and Galloway, were other reiver families, such as Armstrong, Beattie, Bell, Carmichael, Carruthers, Crichton, Douglas, Glendinning, Graham, Henderson, Hunter, Irvine, Jardine, Johnstone, Laidlaw, Lyle, Little, Maxwell, Moffat, and Turner. The royal union of Scotland and England in 1603, under King James VI and I, enabled the law to be enforced along the borders thus breaking the power and influence of the reiving families, some went to fight in foreign wars, others moved to Ireland, while the majority settled under the new regime. The Agricultural Revolution of the eighteenth century was the main reason for out-migration from the Scottish Borders. The restructuring of farming led to large scale evictions or clearances of surplus population. Many such disposed people moved north to the burgeoning industrial towns of the Scottish Lowlands, or south to those in England, while an increasing number went abroad, initially to North America and later to Australasia.

David Dobson

Dundee, Scotland, 2012

The People of the Scottish Borders, 1650-1800

AJ	=	Aberdeen Journal, series
CCMC	=	Colonial Clergy of the Middle Colonies
CL	=	Commissariat of Lauder
CLRO	=	City of London Record Office
F	=	Fastii Ecclesiae Scoticanae
GR	=	Glasgow Records
LC	=	Laing Charters, Edinburgh University
MI	=	Monumental Inscription
NEHGS	=	New England Historical Genealogical Society
NRS	=	National Records of Scotland
P	=	Prisoners of the '45
PCC	=	Prerogative Court of Canterbury
RGS	=	Register of the Great Seal of Scotland
RPCS	=	Register of the Privy Council of Scotland
SEC	=	Scottish Exile Community in the Netherlands, 1660-1690
SHR	=	Services of Heirs, Roxburghshire, 1636-1847
SM	=	Scots Magazine, series
SQR	=	Scottish Quaker Records
TNA	=	The National Archives, London

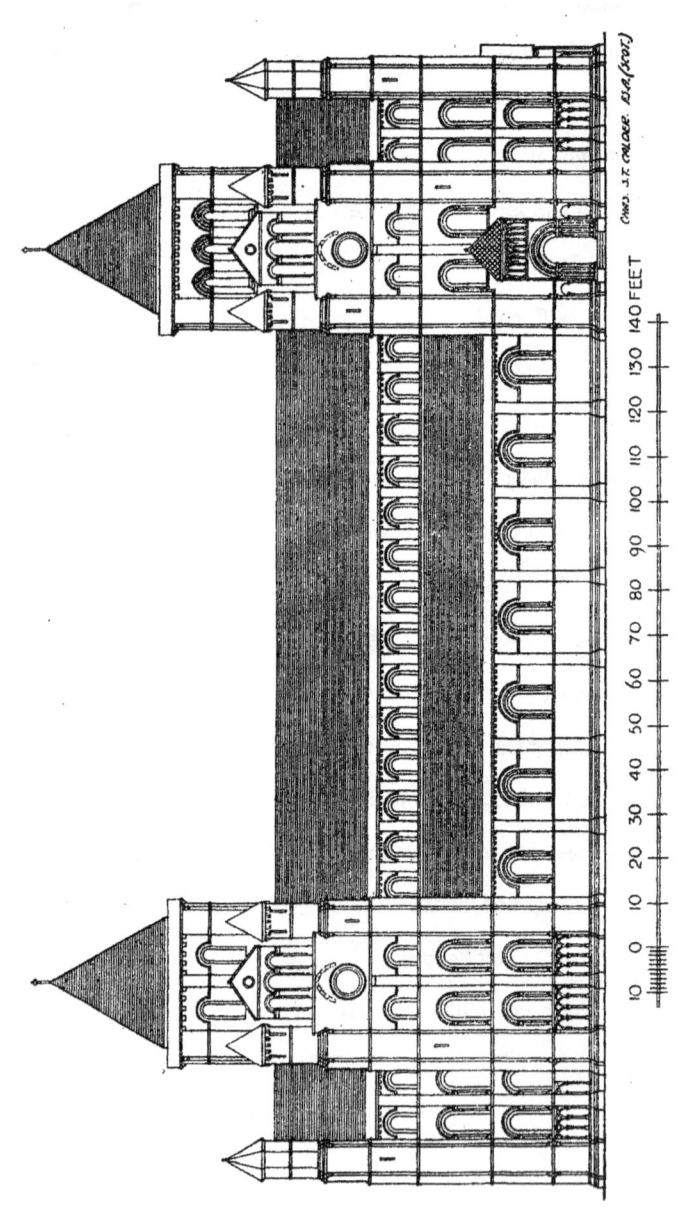

KELSO ABBEY, NORTH ELEVATION,
As it probably appeared in 1517.

South Transept
Melrose Abbey

Ferniehirst Castle nr Jedburgh

X

THE PEOPLE OF THE SCOTTISH BORDERS, 1650-1800

ABERNETHY, GEORGE, a butcher in Duns, testament, 1740. C.L. [NRS]

ABERNETHY, WILLIAM, a tide-surveyor in Eyemouth, testament, 1779. CL. [NRS]

ACKMAN, JAMES, born 1732, died 19 March 1819, his spouse Margaret Glehom, born 1728, died 19 March 1812. [Ayton MI. Berwickshire]

ADAM, MARGARET, widow of John Chatto the younger, a merchant in Kelso, later spouse to Lancelot Brown, a messenger in Kelso, Roxburghshire, versus John Chatto, son of Thomas Chatto, the younger, a merchant in Kelso, 1704. [NRS.CS228.A.1.26]

ADAMS, JOHN, an architect in Edinburgh, heir to Thomas Forbes, eldest son of Thomas Forbes of Thornton who died in January 1769, 1770. [NRS.S/H]

ADAMSON, GEORGE, tenant in Reston Mill, testament, 1764, C.L.[NRS]

ADAMSON, MARGARET, in Mungowalls, testament, 1676, C.L. [NRS]

AINSLIE, ADAM, in Greenlaw, testament, 1733, C.L. [NRS]

AINSLIE, CHARLES, a son of James Ainslie in Longshaw Miln, a sasine, 1763. [NRS.RS18.14.453]

AINSLIE, GEORGE, in Langshaw Miln, a deed, 1759. [NRS.CC18.7.202]

AINSLIE, JAMES, tenant in Muirtown, Longformacus, testament, 1780, C.L. [NRS]

AINSLIE, JOHN, deacon of the cordiners of Jedburgh, deeds, 1715. [NRS.RD4.116.313/700]

AINSLIE, JOHN, a vintner in Jedburgh, a deed, 1715. [NRS.RD2.105.641]

AINSLIE, MARGARET, daughter of James Ainslie late tenant of Mosshouses, died 19 October 1745. [Earlston MI]

AINSLIE, MARGARET, in Jedburgh, a deed, 1758. [NRS.CC18.7.184]

The People of the Scottish Borders, 1650-1800

AINSLIE, ROBERT, of Darnchester, died at Cairnbank on 10 April 1795, his spouse Katharine Whitelaw of Whitelaw in East Lothian, died there 18 December 1803. [Duns MI]

AINSLEY, THOMAS, born 1701, a carpenter from Jedburgh, Roxburghshire, emigrated via London to Maryland in August 1720. [CLRO/AIA]

AINSLIE, THOMAS, a writer and notary in Jedburgh, a deed, 1715. [NRS.RD2.105.897]

AINSLIE, THOMAS, probably from Roxburghshire, emigrated before 1722, a Customs collector in Boston and Quebec, husband of Elizabeth Martin. [NRS.RD4.275.447; RD4.239.11]

AINSLIE, WILLIAM, in Jedburgh, a deed, 1758. [NRS.CC18.7.184]

AIR, JAMES, a fisher in Coldstream, and his wife Agnes Fair, a sasine, 1745. [NRS.RS18.12.164]

AIRE, JOHN, a butcher in Coldstream, testament, 1780, C.L. [NRS]

AIR, PATRICK, a flesher in Coldstream, sasines, 1775/1776. [NRS.RS18.16.416; 17.13]

AIR, ROBERT, a slater in Coldstream, husband of Ann Nisbet who died 8 June 1777. [Lennel MI, Berwickshire]

AIRE, THOMAS, in Coldstream Milne, testament, 1675, C.L. [NRS]

AITCHISON, ALEXANDER, in Newton of Ladykirk, testament, 1681, C.L. [NRS]

AITCHISON, ANDREW, a coppersmith in Kelso, a deed, 1761. [NRS.CC18.7.337]

AITCHISON, JAMES, a schoolmaster in Lauder, sasines, 1752-1773. [NRS.RS18.13.218/515; 16/205/217/244/247]

AITCHISON, THOMAS and ARCHIBALD, in Ladykirk, testament, 1709, C.L. [NRS]

AITKEN, ANDREW, a flesher in Jedburgh, 1770. [NRS.CS228.A.3.48]

AITKEN, JAMES, in Fishwick, testament, 1664, C.L. [NRS]

AITKEN, JAMES, a messenger in Jedburgh, a deed, 1715. [NRS.RD2.105.641]

The People of the Scottish Borders, 1650-1800

AITKEN, JOHN, a flesher in Jedburgh, a deed, 1757. [NRS.CC18.7.121]

AITKEN, WILLIAM, a merchant in Hawick, a deed, 1715. [NRS.RD2.104.390]

AITKEN, WILLIAM, in Ashiesteel, son and heir of John Aitken portioner of Midlem, 1798. [NRS.S/H]

ALEXANDER, ALEXANDER, a wheelwright in Hutton, sasine, 1778. [NRS.RS18.17.227]

ALEXANDER, DANIEL GRAY, born 1812, son of Robert Alexander, died in Virginia City, California, 30 July 1872. [Ayton MI, Berwickshire]

ALEXANDER, GEORGE, in Newton of Coldstream, testament, 1734, C.L. [NRS]

ALEXANDER, JAMES, a merchant in Coldstream, testament, 1681, C.L. [NRS]

ALEXANDER, JOHN, a merchant in Peebles, a deed, 1761. [NRS.CC18.7.338]

ALISON, JOHN, a burgess of Lauder, a sasine, 1772. [NRS.RS18.16.143]

ALLAN, ALEXANDER, a merchant in Lauder, a sasine, 1765. [NRS.RS18.15.153]

ALLAN, DAVID, possibly from Berwickshire, a mason and bricklayer, settled in St Catharine's, Middlesex County, Jamaica, husband of Katherine Drummond, father of David, died 1783 in Jamaica. [NRS.RD2.235.215]

ALLAN, HUGH, born 1683, a meal-maker in Blainslie, died 24 March 1762, husband of Jane Ferlie, born 1680, died 28 February 1749. [Legerwood MI, Berwickshire]

ALLAN, JAMES, grieve to Sir Patrick Hume of Polwarth, baronet and Baillie of Polwarth, died 27 December 1695. [Polwarth MI, Berwickshire]

ALLAN, JAMES, of Paxton, sasines, 1753-1767. [NRS.RS18.13/323; 14/99/100/509; 15/255]

ALLAN, JOHN, born 1639, portioner of Whitson and macebearer to the Earl of Marchmont the Lord High Chancellor of Scotland, died 3 January 1703. [Polwarth MI, Berwickshire]

The People of the Scottish Borders, 1650-1800

ALLAN, JOHN, son of the late Alexander Allan, tenant in Eyemouth and late sailor aboard the Churchill, galley, Captain Olipher, testament, 1717, C.L. [NRS]

ALLAN, JOHN, a merchant and feuar in Duns, testament, 1720, C.L. [NRS]

ALLAN, PATRICK, born 1665, macebearer to Patrick, Earl of Marchmont, Lord High Chancellor of Scotland, died 4 August 1697. [Polwarth MI, Berwickshire]

ALLAN, PATRICK, a wright in Duns, testament, 1731, C.L. [NRS]

ALLAN, RICHARD, a merchant burgess of Lauder, testament, 1722, C.L. [NRS]

ALLAN, RICHARD, a flesher in Kelso, 1770. [NRS.CS228.A.3.48]

ALLAN, ROBERT, a cordiner in Hawick, a deed, 1715. [NRS.RD4.116.313]

ALLAN, ROBERT, a butcher in Kelso, deeds, 1759, 1761. [NRS.CC18.7.214/379]

ALLAN, WALTER, a merchant in Duns, a sasine, 1776. [NRS.RS18.17.3]

ALLAN, WILLIAM, a bailie of Polwarth, testament, 1715, C.L. [NRS]

ALLANSHAW, ALEXANDER, a shoemaker in Eyemouth, a sasine, 1749. [NRS.RS18.12.469]

ALLANSHAW, THOMAS, a shoemaker in Eyemouth, sasines, 1709/1755. [NRS.RS18.13.482]

ANCRUM, MARY, daughter of William Ancrum a merchant in Duns, and spouse to Sir Alexander Cockburn of Langtoun, sasines, 1721-1760. [NRS.RS18.9/415; 10/493; 14/177]

ANCRUM, WILLIAM, a merchant in Duns, testament, 1699, C.L. [NRS]

ANDERSON, ALEXANDER, born 1681, died 16 March 1760, his wife Agnes Simpson, died 20 April 1749. [Earlston MI]

ANDERSON, ANDREW, born 1664, a laborer from Selkirk, emigrated via London to Maryland 5 August 1685. [CLRO/AIA]

ANDERSON, GEORGE, a merchant in Selkirk, a deed, 1715. [NRS.RD2.104.679]

The People of the Scottish Borders, 1650-1800

ANDERSON, ISABELLA, heir to her late husband William Scott in Hawick Shiells, 1793. [NRS.S/H]

ANDERSON, JOHN, a watchmaker in Duns, sasines, 1760-1765. [NRS.RS18.14/227/249; 15/48/126

ANDERSON, JOHN, a breeches maker in Kelso, 1784. [NRS.CS228.A.5.27.1]

ANDERSON, JOHN, in Coldingham, testament, 1787, C.L. [NRS]

ANDERSON, JOHN KIRTON, of Tushielaw, heir to his mother Barbara Anderson of Tushielaw, wife of the late Alexander Kirton a surgeon in Barbados, 1800. [NRS.S/H]

ANDERSON, JOSEPH, born 1739, feuar in Kelso, died 23 December 1819, husband of Alison Kerr, born 1752, died 22 October 1820. [Kelso MI]

ANDERSON, ROBERT, a merchant in Duns, a deed, 1715. [NRS.RD3.146.712]; testament, 1759, C.L. [NRS]

ANDERSON, THOMAS, a seaman in Coldingham, a sasine, 1757. [NRS.RS18.13.517]

ANDERSON, WALTER, a merchant in Kelso, a deed, 1756. [NRS.CC18.7.46]

ANDERSON, WILLIAM, a weaver in Kelso, a Quaker, 1690s. [NRS. Scottish Quaker Records, k.17.89/119]

ANGUS, JEAN, spouse to John Temple a shoemaker in Duns, a sasine, 1729. [NRS.RS18.10.314]

ANSTRUTHER, ISOBEL, spouse to Thomas Tait, in Middle Moristoun, testament, 1683, C.L. [NRS]

ARBUCKLE, JOHN, in Eyemouth, a sasine, 1756. [NRS.RS18.13.500]

ARCHBALD, BETTY, spouse of Thomas Gray in Swinton, a sasine, 1778. [NRS.RS18.17.205]

ARCHER, JAMES, a glover in Duns, a sasine, 1756. [NRS.RS18.13.505]

ARCHER, JAMES, a writer in Greenlaw, testament, 1761, C.L. [NRS]

The People of the Scottish Borders, 1650-1800

ARCHER, THOMAS, in East Gordon, testament, 1681, C.L. [NRS]

ARCHIBALD, ANDREW, in Hume, testament, 1697, C.L. [NRS]

ARMSTRONG, ADAM, in Jedburgh, a deed, 1757. [NRS.CC18.7.65]

ARMSTRONG, ANDREW, a wright in Greenlaw, sasines, 1751-1779. [NRS.RS18.13/135; 17/345/361]

ARMSTRONG, GEORGE, in Berwick, formerly a mason in Paxton, sasines, 1766-1770. [NRS.RS18.15/205/466]

ARMSTRONG, GEORGE, born 1788 in Roxburghshire, emigrated to America 1819, settled in Ovid, New York. [SG.32.3]

ARMSTRONG, JOHN, of Weens, deeds, 1756/1757. [NRS.CC18.7.28/58/107]

ARMSTRONG, ROBERT, from Jedburgh, Roxburghshire, transported from Leith to Barbados 17 April 1666. [ETR.106]

ARMSTRONG, WILLIAM, heir to his grandfather William Armstrong, smith in Kelso, 1705. [NRS.S/H]

ARNEILL, FRANCIS, in Coldingham, a sasine, 1698. [NRS.RS18.5.402]

ARNEILLE, JOHN, in Coldingham, testament, 1669, C.L. [NRS]

ARNOT, JOHN, postmaster at Ayton, testament, 1694, C.L. [NRS]

ARTHURSON, PATRICK, in Duns, a sasine, 1660. [NRS.RS18.4.128]

AUCHENLECK, THOMAS, a surgeon apothecary in Duns, sasines, 1699-1723. [NRS.RS18.5/422; 6/361; 7/490; 9/596]

AULD, DAVID, a merchant in Coldstream, sasines, 1774-1775. [NRS.RS18.16/356/375]

AULD, ROBERT, a cooper in Coldstream, a sasine, 1779. [NRS.RS18.17.333]

AYMERS, THOMAS, a wright in Nunlands, testament, 1730, C.L. [NRS]

AYTON, RALPH, a soldier, sasines, 1769/1770. [NRS.RS18.15/374/433]

BAILLIE, Dame GRIZELL, of Jerviswood, testament, 1759, C.L. [NRS]

The People of the Scottish Borders, 1650-1800

BAILLIE, JOHN, son of Alexander Baillie of Callends, Peebles-shire, a surgeon, from the Clyde aboard the Rising Sun bound for Darien 18 August 1699, died at Darien, testament, 1707. [NRS.CC8.8.83]

BAILLIE, ROBERT, of Jerviswood, a sasine, 1688. [NRS.RS18.5.39]

BAIRD, Sir JAMES, of Saughtonhall, sasines, 1764. [NRS.RS18.15/9/12/14/18]

BAIRNSFATHER, JOHN, tenant in Knocks, later in Duns, a deed, 1715. [NRS.RD4.116.1288]

BAIRNSFATHER, WILLIAM, in Duns, a sasine, 1695. [NRS.RS18.5.292]

BALD, JEAN, spouse of Henry Dounie a carrier in Coldingham, a sasine, 1744. [NRS.RS18.12.71]

BALD, WILLIAM, in West Gordon, testament, 1653, C.L. [NRS]

BALDERSTONE, WILLIAM, a physician in Berwick, sasines, 1759-1775. [NRS.RS18.14/102; 15/421;16/399]

BALFOUR, JAMES, born in Duns, minister at Eccles from 1687 to 1691. [F.2.13]

BALFOUR, JOHN, born in Bowden, 25 September 1798, son of Reverend William Balfour and his wife Mary Mein, died in Boston, USA, 15 August 1844. [F.2.172]

BALFOUR, ROBERT, a notary in Duns, a sasine, 1663. [NRS.RS18.1.64]

BALGARNO, HELEN, spouse to Peter Broun feuar in Duns, a sasine, 1670. [NRS.RS18.2.248]

BALLANTYNE, DAVID, a merchant in Coldstream, sasines, 1753-1775. [NRS.RS18.13/313; 15/350; 16/150/392]

BALMUR, ROBERT, a carrier in Hawick, deeds, 1757/1761. [NRS.CC18.7.101/306]

BALMER, STEPHEN, born 1687, late tenant in Longnewton, died 18 January 1738, his spouse Janet Walker, born 1686, died 30 September 1756. [Longnewton MI]

The People of the Scottish Borders, 1650-1800

BALMUR, WALTER, in Longnewton, a deed, 1757. [NRS.CC18.7.101]

BANE, THOMAS, in Teinside, a deed, 1761. [NRS.CC18.7.343]

BANNATYNE, MARGARET, spouse of Alexander Douglas minister at Coldingham, a sasine, 1695. [NRS.RS18.5.294]

BANNATYNE, WILLIAM, minister at Yarrow from 1711 until is death on 17 January 1753; husband of (1) Euphan Mure, (2) Isobel Lundie, parents of Archibald, and Jean. [F.2.197]

BARBOUR, GEORGE, a sasine, 1663. [NRS.RS18.1.128]

BARCLAY, Miss, a shopkeeper in Kelso, 1785. [NRS.E326.4.1]

BARNS, DAVID, feuar and gardener in Duns, testament, 1766, C.L. [NRS]

BARNES, ROBERT, a dyer in Kelso, a Quaker, 1690s. [NRS. Scottish Quaker Records, E.11.3/5; K17.88/119]

BARROWMAN, JANET, daughter of Martin Barrowman in Shiplaw, and spouse to John Purves, son of Thomas Purves of Bridgend, Earlston, 1675. [NRS.RS18.3.271]

BATHGATE, ALISON, widow of John Murray of Wooplaw, testament, 1729, C.L. [NRS]

BATHGATE, SIMON, in Langhop, testament, 1676, C.L. [NRS]

BAXTER, CHARLES, a merchant in Edinburgh, heir to his brother Thomas Baxter a writer in Jedburgh, 1799. [NRS.S/H]

BEATSON, THOMAS, feuar in Duns, testament, 1692, C.L. [NRS]

BEATTIE, MARGARET, in Leshaugh, a deed, 1759. [NRS.CC18.7.216]

BEATTIE, MARION, in Keshaugh, a deed, 1759. [NRS.CC18.7.216]

BEATTIE, RICHARD, in Leshaugh, a deed, 1759. [NRS.CC18.7.216]

BEATTIE, ROBERT, a merchant in Langholm, a deed, 1761. [NRS.CC18.7.306]

The People of the Scottish Borders, 1650-1800

BEINSTOUN, ISOBEL, spouse to George Ridpath in Horndean, testament, 1664, C.L. [NRS]

BELCHES, ALISON, a servant from Lintlaw, Berwickshire, transported July 1744. [NRS.HCR.I.72]

BELL, ALEXANDER, tenant in Greenlaw Milne, testament, 1748, C.L. [NRS]

BELL, ALISON, in Dunse, testament, 1758, C.L. [NRS]

BELL, ANDREW, in Oxnam, a deed, 1757. [NRS.CC18.7.119]

BELL, ANDREW, at Spylaw, a deed, 1757. [NRS.CC18.7.94]

BELL, GEORGE, a merchant in Coldstream, a deed, 1715. [NRS.RD4.116.674]; testament, 1746, C.L. [NRS]

BELL, GEORGE, a wright in Langtoun, a deed, 1757. [NRS.CC18.7.109]

BELL, JAMES, son of Andrew Bell of Bellford, a deed, 1715. [NRS.RD3.146.318]

BELL, JAMES, in Whitton, a deed, 1760. [NRS.CC18.7.295]

BELL, JOHN, in Hollie, son of William Bell in Smailholm, a deed, 1715. [NRS.RD4.117.222]

BELL, ROBERT, in Coldingham, a dragoon of the Royal Scots Greys, testament, 1744, C.L. [NRS]

BELL, WILLIAM, born 1661, an indweller in Dryburgh, died 26 September 1734, his spouse Agnes Hatlie (?), born 1662, died 20 December 1719. [Dryburgh MI]

BELL, WILLIAM, born 1701, a book-seller from Berwickshire, a Jacobite transported from Liverpool aboard the <u>Veteran</u> bound for the Leeward Islands 5 May 1747, landed on Martinique in June 1747. [TNA.SP36.102][P.2.32]

BENNET, ANDREW, of Chesters, Roxburghshire, born 1687, died 16 July 1745, his spouse Dorothy Collingwood, born 1719, died July 1761. [Ancrum MI] [NRS.CS228.B.2.95]

BENNET, WILLIAM, born before 1671, a forger from Roxburghshire, transported 1751. [SM.13.501]

The People of the Scottish Borders, 1650-1800

BERTHAM, ALEXANDER, born 1795 in Berwickshire, died in Augusta, Georgia, 27 November 1827. [Georgia Courier, 29.11.1827]

BERTRAM, JAMES, in Peebles, a bond, 1769. [NRS.RD4.207.204]

BERTRAM, JOHN, born 1684, tenant in Cockburn, died 15 September 1772, his wife Mary Dods, born 1693, died 23 April 1778. [Cranshaws MI, Berwickshire]

BERTRAM, WILLIAM, tenant in Raburn, testament, 1713, C.L. [NRS]

BEST, JOHN, in Town Rule, a deed, 1759. [NRS.CC18.7.205]

BEST, ROBERT, in Bedrule, a deed, 1758. [NRS.CC18.7.190]

BEVERICH, JOHN, sometime in Dunglass Milne, later in Houburn Milne, Coldingham, testament, 1724, C.L. [NRS]

BICHET, ISOBEL, spouse to Thomas Tumter, in Ligertwood, testament, 1664, C.L. [NRS]

BICKET, THOMAS, heir to his grandfather Thomas Bicket, portioner of Bowden, 1692. [SHR.12]

BLACK, ROBERT, miller, died 12 February 1726. [Ancrum MI, Roxburghshire]

BLACK, WILLIAM, schoolmaster at Ancrum, died 9 May 1777. [Ancrum MI, Roxburghshire]

BLACKADDER, ALEXANDER, in Blackadder, and his spouse Isobel Carmichael, testament, 1711, C.L. [NRS]

BLACKADDER, JOHN, tenant in Edram, testament, 1795, C.L. [NRS]

BLACKIE, ALEXANDER, born 1723, a gardener in Kelso, died 10 January 1803, his spouse Agnes Stevenson died 11 September 1818. [Kelso MI]

BLACKIE, JAMES, a wright and portioner of Craigsfoord, testaments, 1750/1751, C.L. [NRS]

BLACKIE, ROBERT, born 1744, surgeon in Coldstream, died 4 July 1780, husband of Margaret Denholm. [Coldstream MI, Berwickshire]

The People of the Scottish Borders, 1650-1800

BLAIKIE, JAMES, son of James Blaikie in Galashiels, Selkirkshire, a thief, transported in October 1752. [AJ.250]

BLAIKIE, JAMES, from Eccles, Berwickshire, a member of the Scots Charitable Society of Boston, 1775. [SCS]

BLAIR, JOHN, in Edmisden, testament, 1680, C.L. [NRS]

BLAIR, PETER, minister at Jedburgh, 1661 until his death on 7 May 1673, husband of Mary Hamilton, parents of Jean. [F.2.126]

BLAIR, PETER, from Cockburnspath, Berwickshire, settled in Salem, Massachusetts, married Sarah Baker in Marblehead on 5 October 1752. [Imm.NE.220]

BLAKIE, ANDREW, tenant of Faugh-hill, died 1760 aged 75, spouse of Elisabeth Scott born 1682, died 1758. [Longnewton MI, Roxburghshire]

BLAKITER, GEORGE, born 1718, died 11 June 1778, his spouse Agnes Brown, born 1716, died 6 December 1779. [Lennel MI, Berwickshire]

BLEAKY, JOHN, a wright in Jedburgh, a deed, 1761. [NRS.CC18.7.369]

BLEAKIE, JOHN, a shopkeeper in Kelso, 1785. [NRS.E326.4.1]

BLINSHALL, DAVID, minister at Lamington, a deed, 1715. [NRS.RD4.117.313]

BLYTH, JOHN, late in Clarilaw, died 5 May 1763, his spouse Isabel Laidlaw, born 1685, died July 1780, parents of Andrew Blyth, born 1722, tenant in Nethertoafts, died 4 March 1800. [Cavers MI]

BOAG, ANDREW, a shoemaker in Jedburgh, a deed, 1756. [NRS.CC18.7.45]

BOAG, PATRICK, of Burnhouse, Commissar of Peebles, a deed, 1715. [NRS.RD4.116.1173]

BOGUE, ALEXANDER, of Greenburn, testament, 1783, C.L. [NRS]

BOGUE, WILLIAM, born 1717, portioner of Auchencraw, died 1780, husband of Elizabeth Murray, parents of George Bogue, born 1795, a surgeon in Jamaica, died 5 September 1817. [Coldingham MI, Berwickshire]

The People of the Scottish Borders, 1650-1800

BOLL, JAMES, son and heir of John Boll, tenant in Nether Calsay, Roxburghshire, 1710. [NRS.S/H]

BOLL, JOHN, a baxter in Jedburgh, deeds, 1756, 1760. [NRS.CC18.7.45/301]

BONNINGTON, WILLIAM, portioner of Bowden, a deed,1759. [NRS.CC18.7.226]

BOOG, ALEXANDER, portioner of Auchencraw, testament, 1730, C.L. [NRS]

BOOKLESS, GEORGE, born 1678, died 7 June 1748. [St Helens on the Lea MI, Berwickshire]

BOOKLESS, MARY, widow of James Tait, tenant in Boushiell, testament, 1732, C.L. [NRS]

BOOKLESS, WILLIAM, portioner of Eyemouth, testament, 1719, C.L. [NRS]

BORTHWICK, ANDREW, heir to his father William Borthwick in Trowmilne, 1693. [NRS.S/H]

BORTHWICK, FRANCIS, of Hartside, testament, 1706, C.L. [NRS]

BORTHWICK, GEORGE, deacon of the shoemakers of Jedburgh, and his son John, a deed, 1715. [NRS.RD4.116.700]

BORTHWICK, JOHN, of Stow, a deed, 1715. [NRS.RD2.104.582]

BORTHWICK, JOHN, of Trottingshaw, testaments, 1740, 1741, 1743, 1745, C.L. [NRS]

BORTHWICK, JOHN, a merchant in Jedburgh, a deed, 1760. [NRS.CC18.7.300]

BOSTON, HENRY, from Ettrick, Selkirkshire, to Maryland 1640, possibly in Accomack County, Virginia, by 1649, husband of Anne ..., parents of Isaac, settled in Somerset County, Maryland, died 1670. [CF.3.54][BLG.2572]

BOSTON, JAMES, portioner of Gallonside, a deed, 1756. [NRS.CC18.7.53]; eldest son of the deceased James Boston of Gattonside, heir to his uncle Andrew Boston, a portioner there, 1764. [NRS.S/H]

The People of the Scottish Borders, 1650-1800

BOSTON, ROBERT, born in Kelso, Roxburghshire, 1779, a slater in Kelso son and heir of John Boston portioner and slater in Gattonside, 1796, [NRS.S/H], a slater in New York from 1806 until his death on 11 December 1813, naturalised 17 April 1811. [St Andrew's Society of New York.II.7]

BOSWELL, ROBERT and MARY, children of Robert Boswell, tobacconist in Jedburgh, and Mary Wright his first spouse, heir to their father, 1769. [NRS.S/H]

BOWDEN, JAMES, a cordiner in Kelso, a deed, 1715. [NRS.RD4.116.700]

BOWER, NICOLL, portioner of Newtoun, deeds, 1756/1757/1759. [NRS.CC18.7.52/118/120/202]

BOWHILL, JOHN, a watchmaker in London, heir to Thomas Bowhill, gardener in Kelso and portioner of Melrose, 1769. [NRS.S/H]

BOWIE, BESSIE, in Coldstream, testament, 1662, C.L. [NRS]

BOWIE, JOHN, born 1687, a smith in Cavers, Roxburghshire, died 13 April 1757, his wife Mary Scott, born 1689, died 12 April 1749. [Cavers MI]

BOWMAKER, ALISON, spouse to George King, in Whitsumlaws, testament, 1653, C.L. [NRS]

BOWMAKER, JOHN, in Fishwick, testament, 1676, C.L. [NRS]

BOWMAKER, ROBERT, minister at Abbey St Bathans, 1682 to his death in 1697. [F.2.2]

BOWMAKER, ROBERT, DD, born 1737, minister at Duns 1769-1797, died 11 March 1797, husband of May Watson, born 30 April 1748, died 20 October 1816. [Duns MI][F.2.10]

BOYD, JOHN, tenant in the barony of Mertoun, heir to his uncle Robert Boyd, baxter and bailie of Hawick, 1768. [NRS.S/H]

BOYD, ROBERT, in Blauod, testament, 1689, C.L. [NRS]

BRACK, CHRISTIAN, the elder, in Polwarth, testament, 1673, C.L. [NRS]

BRACK, WILLIAM, a farmer in Crossrig, testament, 1700, C.L. [NRS]

The People of the Scottish Borders, 1650-1800

BRACK, WILLIAM, only son of William Brack, portioner of Smailholm, and the late Agnes Hutchison his spouse, eldest daughter of the deceased William Hutchison, portioner of Smailholm, heir to his grandfather the said William Hutchison, 1765. [NRS.S/H]

BRAIDIE, ELSPETH, spouse of Philip Haistie, in Peilwalls, testament, 1682, C.L. [NRS]

BRAIDIE, ROBERT, born 1713, feuar in Duns, died 4 March 1783. [Duns MI]

BRAIMER, MARGARET, widow of John Mow, of East Mains, testament, 1751, C.L. [NRS]

BRAND, ZACHARIAH, in Whytmyre, and his daughter Janet Brand, testament, 1677, C.L. [NRS]

BREWES, JOHN, tacksman of Kelso Mills, heir to his father James Brewes, late tenant in Kelso Mills, 1769. [SHR.30]

BREWHOUSE, ISABEL, born 1721, spouse to James Jamieson tenant in Museridge, died 14 June 1767.

BREWHOUSE, JOHN, deacon of the Smiths Trade in Jedburgh, a deed, 1757. [NRS.CC18.7.120]

BRIDGES, SUSANNA, in Home, testament, 1684, C.L. [NRS]

BRIGGS, JANET, widow of Andrew Hardie, tenant in Fauns, testament, 1736, C.L. [NRS]

BRODIE, ANDREW, schoolmaster of Abbey St Bathuns, testament, 1736, C.L. [NRS]

BRODIE, JOHN, a mealmaker in Maxmill, testament, 1750, C.L. [NRS]

BRODIE, THOMAS, born 1740, tenant in Ayton Mill, died 24 July 1812. [Ayton MI, Berwickshire]

BROKIE, THOMAS, born 1705, tenant in Bemerside, died 6 January 1776. [Dryburgh Abbey MI, Berwickshire]

BROOMFIELD, JAMES, tenant in Hiltounhill, testament, 1749, C.L. [NRS]

The People of the Scottish Borders, 1650-1800

BROOMFIELD, STEPHEN, of Nethermains, testament, 1763, C.L. [NRS]

BROTHERSTONES, ALEXANDER, late bailie of Lauder, testament, 1712, C.L. [NRS]

BROTHERSTONES, THOMAS, a baxter in Fauns, testament, 1736, C.L. [NRS]

BROWN, ALEXANDER, a cordiner in Kelso, a deed, 1715. [NRS.RD4.116.700]

BROWN, ANDREW, a wright in Kelso, a deed, 1715. [NRS.RD4.116.505]

BROWN, ANDREW, a carrier in Hawick, a deed, 1758. [NRS.CC18.7.142]

BROWN, DANIEL, an undertaker in Melrose, a deed, 1758. [NRS.CC18.7.186]

BROWN, DAVID, educated at Edinburgh University, minister at Greenlaw 1707, at Gordon 1708, and at Selkirk from 1725 until his death on 12 March 1753; husband of (1) Christian Henderson, parents of William, (2) Janet Scott, parents of Mary. [F.2.195]

BROWN, GEORGE, born 1718, a tailor in Chirnside, died 8 August 1786. [Chirnside MI, Berwickshire]

BROWN, GUSTAVUS, M.D., in St Mary's County, Maryland, grandson and heir of Gustavus Brown, M.D., OF Mainside, parish of Hownam, 1792. [NRS.S/H]

BROWN, JAMES, servant to George Gordon, of Gordonbank, testament, 1760, C.L. [NRS]

BROWN, JAMES MURRAY, born in Kilmabreck, 6 April 1767, son of Reverend Samuel Brown and his wife Margaret Smith, died in Virginia. [F.2.368]

BROWN, JANET, born 1727, spouse of the late Robert Wilson a merchant in Mellarstain, died 25 April 1808. [Earlston MI, Berwickshire]

BROWN, JOHN, in Blackadder New Mains, testament, 1708, C.L. [NRS]

BROWN, JOHN, a cordiner in Kelso, a deed, 1715. [NRS.RD4.116.313]

BROWN, JOHN, a surgeon from Coldstream, Berwickshire, settled in Williamsburg, Virginia, by 1753, father of Robert and Charles; died in Virginia, 1727, testament, 1730, Edinburgh . [NRS.RS18.13.314; CC8.8.93; S/H.1731]

BROWN, JOHN, in Langtoun, a deed, 1760. [NRS.CC18.7.302]

BROWN, JOSEPH, a writer in Jedburgh, a deed, 1758. [NRS.CC18.7.141]

BROWN, ROBERT, huntsman in Chatterdenfoord, testament, 1731, C.L. [NRS]

BROWN, THOMAS, a surgeon in Broom, a deed, 1761. [NRS.CC18.7.353]

BROWN, WILLIAM, a merchant in Jedburgh, a deed, 1760. [NRS.CC18.7.233]

BROWN, Mrs, in Selkirk, 1783. [NRS.E326.1.210]

BROWNFIELD, ROBERT, a tailor in Kello, testament, 1721, C.L. [NRS]

BROWNLEE, JANET, spouse to John Burne, violer in Earlston, testament, 1653, C.L. [NRS]

BRUNTFIELD, ROBERT, in Westraw of Greenlaw, testament, 1691, C.L. [NRS]

BRYDEN, JOHN, in Appletreeleaves, a deed, 1756. [NRS.CC18.7.28]

BRYDEN, WILLIAM, a merchant in Galashiels, a deed, 1715. [NRS.RD4.117.596]

BRYSON, JOHN, a weaver in Hawick, deeds, 1761. [NRS.CC18.7.345/377]

BUCK, JOB, a shipmaster in Eyemouth, testament, 1753, C.L. [NRS]

BUCKHAM, JOHN, of Bush, heir to his father John Buckham, tenant in Bedrule, 1791. [NRS.S/H]

BULLERWALL, JAMES, schoolmaster in Duns, testaments, 1699/1719, C.L. [NRS]

BUNYAN, ANDREW, minister at Howgate, heir to his uncle James Bunyan, mason and portioner of Newstead, 1778. [NRS.S/H]

BURGEON, JOHN, tenant in Crumrigg, testament, 1777, C.L. [NRS]

BURN, GEORGE, in Duns, testament, 1663, C.L. [NRS]

BURN, ROBERT, a cordiner in Kelso, a deed, 1715. [NRS.RD4.116.313]

The People of the Scottish Borders, 1650-1800

BURN, ROBERT, an innkeeper in Kelso, heir to his brother James Burn, grandson of the deceased Robert Burn the Convenor of the Trades of Kelso, 1798. [NRS.S/H]

BURNET, DAVID, in Earlston, testament, 1653, C.L. [NRS]

BURNET, ROBERT, a preacher of the Gospel and governor to the children of the late Sir Alexander Don of Newton, testament, 1749, C.L. [NRS]

BUSBY, AGNES, in Kelso, died 15 May 1685, sister of Andrew Busby a wright. [NRS.Scottish Quaker Records, k17.118]

BUSBY, ANDREW, a wright in Kelso, husband of Elizabeth Lamb, parents of Agnes, and Joseph, 1680s. [NRS. Scottish Quaker Records, k.17]

BUSBY, JANE, in Maxwellhaugh, died 1672. [NRS.Scottish Quaker Records.k17]

BUTE, JOHN, in Home, testament, 1710, C.L. [NRS]

BUTTER, HELEN, daughter of the late John Butter, formerly of Gormack, testament, 1781, C.L. [NRS]

CAIRNCROSS, ELIZABETH, of Hilslap, deeds, 1759. [NRS.CC18.7.190/194]

CAIRNS, ELSPETH, in East Brockles, testament, 1756, C.L. [NRS]

CALDCLEUCH, JAMES, in East Nisbet, testament, 1673, C.L. [NRS]

CALDER, PETER, born 1695, died 7 October 1770, husband of Margaret Thompson. [Abbey St Bathans MI, Berwickshire]

CALDERWOOD, MARGARET, in Poltoun, a deed, 1761. [NRS.CC18.7.308]

CALDERWOOD, THOMAS, of Poltoun, a deed, 1761. [NRS.CC18.7.308]

CALDWELL, DAVID, portioner of Coldstream, a deed, 1715. [NRS.RD3.145.375]

CALLENDAR, JANET, widow o Patrick Forton, tenant in Earlscleugh, testament, 1736, C.L. [NRS]

CALVERT, SAMUEL, a clothier in Ednam, 1784. [NRS.CS228.A.5.27.1]

The People of the Scottish Borders, 1650-1800

CAMPBELL, DOUGALL, late cornet of the Royal Grey Dragoons, testament, 1730, C.L. [NRS]

CAMPBELL, JAMES, of Nether Stichill, died 1678, father of Catherine, John, Annabel, Isaac, and Sarah. [NRS. Scottish Quaker Records.k17]

CAMPBELL, JEAN, relict of Dr John Taylor, of Pitcairly, Longformacus, testament, 1770, C.L. [NRS]

CAMPBELL, JOHN, born 1672, minister at Cranshaws from 1706 until his death in 1759, spouse of Elizabeth Craig. [F.2.6]

CAMPBELL, MALCOLM, late servant to John Carr of Nisbet, testament, 1776, C.L. [NRS]

CAMPBELL, MARGARET, relict of John Callendar a burgess of Lauder, testament, 1678, C.L. [NRS]

CAMPBELL, WILLIAM, born 10 January 1737, son of William Campbell the Customs surveyor in Kirkcaldy, educated at Edinburgh University, minister at Lilliesleaf from 1760 until his death on 28 September 1804; husband of Margaret Home. [F.2.183]

CANARIES, JAMES, educated at St Andrews, minister at Selkirk, 1685-1690, husband of Anne Erskine. [F.2.194]

CARFRAE, JANET, relict of James Scott tenant in Hoprigg, testament, 1768, C.L. [NRS]

CARRE, ALEXANDER, of Cavers, son of John Carre of Cavers, heir to his brother John Carre last of Cavers, 1799. [NRS.S/H]

CARRE, JOHN, of Cavers at West Nisbet, Edram, testaments, 1738, 1740, 1741, 1742, C.L. [NRS]

CARRUTHERS, GILBERT, merchant in Leidgerwood, testament, 1693, C.L. [NRS]

CARSE, GAVIN, born 1802, died in Coldstream on 12 January 1782, his wife Alison ....., born 1702, died 6 February 1772. [Lennel MI, Berwickshire]

CARSE, WILLIAM, in Skamure, testament, 1679, C.L. [NRS]

The People of the Scottish Borders, 1650-1800

CARTER, JASPER, tenant in Westruther, testament, 1742, C.L. [NRS]

CARTER, JOHN, tenant in Westruther, testament, 1781, C.L. [NRS]

CARTER, NICOL, in Earlston, testament, 1757, C.L. [NRS]

CASSE, ALEXANDER, parson of Polwarth, testament, 1652, C.L. [NRS]

CASTILLAW, ALISON, spouse to Robert Aitkin in Foulden, testament, 1672, C.L. [NRS]

CHALLANDER, JOHN, a burgess of Lauder, testament, 1670, C.L. [NRS]

CHAMBERS, ANDREW, in Pilmoor, testament, 1676, C.L. [NRS]

CHAMBERS, MARGARET, in East Gordon, spouse to Robert Trotter, testament, 1670, C.L. [NRS]

CHARTERIS, ADAM, late tenant in Lambden, testament, 1736, C.L. [NRS]

CHARTERIS, JOHN, a beggar, sometime in Rumilton Law, testament, 1675, C.L. [NRS]

CHATTO, JAMES, a shoemaker in Newcastle, heir to his father Thomas Chatto a shoemaker in Kelso, 1779. [SHR.35]

CHATTO, JOHN, a feuar in Kelso, a deed, 1715. [NRS.RD4.117.913]

CHATTO, THOMAS, bailie of Kelso, a deed, 1715. [NRS.RD4.116.781]

CHATTO, WILLIAM, a merchant in Kelso, deeds, 1715. [NRS.RD2.104.629; RD4.116.143]

CHIRNSIDE, ANDREW, born 1754, wright at Duns Castle, died 10 June 1803, his spouse Isabella Lidster, born 1763, died 12 May 1803. [Duns MI, Berwiskshire]

CHIRNSIDE, DAVID, in Swinton Mylne, testament, 1668, C.L. [NRS]

CHIRNSIDE, DAVID, born 1725, tenant in Little Dean, died 21 November 1777, his spouse Alison Jamieson, born 1747, died 2 March 1822. [Coldingham MI, Berwickshire]

CHIRNSIDE, NINIAN, in East Nisbet, testament, 1653, C.L. [NRS]

The People of the Scottish Borders, 1650-1800

CHISHOLM, JOHN, educated at Edinburgh University, minister at Lilliesleaf from 1674 to 1689, died in Edinburgh 12 February 1701, aged about 58, father of Robert, Eupham, and Esther. [F.2.182]

CHISHOLM, MARGARET, eldest daughter of Walter Chisholm of Parkhill and spouse of William Ainslie bailie of Jedburgh, a deed, 1715. [NRS.RD4.117.250]

CHISHOLM, MARK, of Parkhill, a deed, 1756. [NRS.CC18.7.36]

CHISHOLM, THOMAS, in Selkirk, 1783. [NRS.E326.1.210]

CHISHOLM, WALTER, a merchant in Selkirk, husband of Margaret Leithead, a deed, 1715. [NRS.RD2.105.343]

CHRISLEY, JAMES, born 1712, a clerk from Selkirk, emigrated via London to Jamaica in November 1736. [CLRO/AIA]

CHRISTIE, ALEXANDER, a writer in Duns, testament, 1734, C.L. [NRS]

CHRISTISON, ALEXANDER, portioner of Hutton, testament, 1732, C.L. [NRS]

CLAPPERTON, JANET, spouse of Andrew Lees tenant in Whitlaw, testament, 1753, C.L. [NRS]

CLAPPERTON, JOHN, son of Rev. John Clapperton in Ednam, educated at Edinburgh University 1642, minister at Yarrow from 1666 until his death in 1679; husband of Margaret Learmonth, parents of Samuel, John, Richard, Thomas, James, Jean, Margaret and Elizabeth. [F.2.196]

CLARK, ADAM, in Greenlaw, testament, 1720, C.L. [NRS]

CLERK, JAMES, a flesher in Jedburgh, a deed, 1759. [NRS.CC18.7.228]

CLARK, JOHN, born 1739, feuar in Kelso, died 17 October 1802, his spouse Margaret Litster, born 1746, died in July 1796, children John, born 1768, Isobel, born 1782, died 1788, and David, born 1771, a tailor in Kelso, died 23 April 1797. [Kelso MI]

CLARK, ROBERT, smith in Langtoun, testament, 1720, C.L. [NRS]

CLEGHORN, ABIMELECH, in Newton of Foulden, testament, 1653, C.L. [NRS]

The People of the Scottish Borders, 1650-1800

CLEGHORN, JAMES, the elder, in Foulden, testament, 1676, C.L. [NRS]

CLINKSCALES, ROBERT, of Otterburn, testament, 1693, C.L. [NRS]

CLINKSCALES, THOMAS, in Wedderburn Mylne, testament, 1652, C.L. [NRS]

CLUNIE, DAVID, minister at Cockburnspath, testament, 1703, C.L. [NRS]

COCKBURN, Sir ALEXANDER, of Langtoun, testament, 1741, C.L. [NRS]

COCKBURN, CORNELIUS, in Salterpath, Duns, testament, 1746, C.L. [NRS]

COCKBURN, HENRY, born 1718, smith in Weddertie, died 16 April 1798, wife Isobel Hardie born 1719, died 15 April 1794.[Westruther MI, Berwickshire]

COCKBURN, JAMES, son of Henry Cockburn of Channelkirk, minister at Abbey St Bathans, 1664-1674. [F.2.2]

COCKBURN, JOHN, a mason from Kelso, Roxburghshire, emigrated via Leith to East New Jersey in 1684, settled in Perth Amboy. [Insh#276]

COCKBURN, JOHN, tenant of the east end of Chirnside, tenant, 1757, C.L. [NRS]

COCKBURN, WALTER, in Harden, deeds, 1757. [NRS.CC18.7.86/118]

COCKBURN, WILLIAM, a merchant in Aytoun, second son of Sir Alexander Cockburn of Langtoun, testaments, 1731, 1732, 1764, C.L. [NRS]

COCHRANE, NICOL, a candlemaker in Jedburgh, a deed, 1715. [NRS.RD4.116.346]

COLDEN, ALEXANDER, son of Rev. Robert Colden, minister at Enniscorthy, Ireland, minister at Bunkle from 1690 to 1693, at Duns from 1693 to 1700. [F.2.5/9]

COLDEN, JAMES, minister at Whitsome, testament, 1762, C.L. [NRS]

COLDWALLS, DAVID, bailie of Coldstream, testament, 1743, C.L. [NRS]

COLLACE, ANDREW, born 1591, minister at Duns from 1663 until his death in 1664. [F.2.9]

COLTHERD, FRANCIS, in Chisholm, a deed, 1758. [NRS.CC18.7.150]

The People of the Scottish Borders, 1650-1800

COLTHERD, WALTER, in Borthickburn, a deed, 1758. [NRS.CC18.7.179]

CONSTABLE, CHARLES, of Moorhall, testament, 1773, C.L. [NRS]

COOK, GEORGE, born 1725, feuar in Swinton, died 16 December 1795. [Swinton MI, Berwickshire]

COOK, GEORGE FREDERICK, born in Berwick-on-Tweed 1755, a tragedian, died in New York on 26 September 1812. [Gentleman's Magazine.82.494]

COOK, JOHN, born 1628, minister at Eccles 1663-1689, died 1691. [F.2.13]

COOK, JOHN, in Whitsome, testament, 1754, C.L. [NRS]

COOPER, ..., in Selkirk, 1783. [NRS.E326.1.210]

CORMACK, DANIEL, born 1745, a feuar in Coldingham, died 22 December 1802. [Coldingham MI, Berwickshire]

CORSAR, ALEXANDER, a butcher in Duns, a deed, 1715. [NRS.RD3.145.198]

CORSAR, ALEXANDER, a drover in Duns, deeds, 1715. [NRS.RD3.144.496; RD4.117.903]

CORSAR, GEORGE, in Duns, a deed, 1715. [NRS.RD4.117.916]

CORSAR, GEORGE, a drover in Duns, a deed, 1715. [NRS.RD4.117.903]

CORSER, GEORGE, a baxter and feuar in Kelso, a deed, 1758. [NRS.CC18.7.138]

CORSAR, JAMES, in Duns, a deed, 1715. [NRS.RD4.117.916]

CORSAR, JOHN, a drover in Duns, a deed, 1715. [NRS.RD3.144.496]

CORSNIP, JAMES, a butcher in Duns, sasines, 1778. [NRS.RS18.17.211/212/221]

CORSNIP, ROBERT, a portioner in Home, and his spouse Janet Sked, a sasine, 1780. [NRS.RS18.17.433]

COSSAR, ALEXANDER, a feuar and drover in Duns, testaments, 1763/1764, C.L. [NRS]

COSSAR, GEORGE, a butcher in Duns, testament, 1760, C.L. [NRS]

The People of the Scottish Borders, 1650-1800

COSSAR, ROBERT, a merchant in Coldingham, testament, 1723, C.L. [NRS]

COSSAR, WALTER, born 1733, a horse-dealer in Duns, died in January 1776, his spouse Jean Wait, born 1721, died in July 1776. [Duns MI, Berwickshire]

COTTEM, ISOBELL, daughter of Henry Cottem in Coldingham, and spouse of James Dounie in Hutton, Berwickshire, a sasine, 1688. [NRS.RS18.5.57]

COUPAR, MATTHEW, minister at Lilliesleaf from 1691 to 1695. [F.2.182]

COURTNEY, ELIZABETH, relict of David Stark minister at Stitchell, a sasine, 1688. [NRS.RS18.5.41]

COURTNEY, THOMAS, minister at Ashkirk, Selkirkshire, in 1667. [F.2.169]

COURTNEY, THOMAS, from Foggo, a member of the Scots Society of Boston, 1770. [NEHGS]

COUSTON, JANET, spouse to Mark Loch in Swinton, testament, 1674, C.L. [NRS]

COUTTS, FRANCES, spouse of John Stuart the younger of Allanbank, Berwickshire, a sasine, 1780. [NRS.RS18..17.427]

COW, HELEN, spouse to George Anderson in Ross, testament, 1653, C.L. [NRS]

COWAN, DAVID, in New Ladykirk, testament, 1703, C.L. [NRS]

COWAN, ROBERT, in Borthickburn, a deed, 1758. [NRS.CC18.7.179]

COWE, JAMES, born 1722, gardener in Chirnside, died 15 October 1806, his wife Isabel Paxton, born 1821, died 16 April 1807. [Chirnside MI, Berwickshire]

COWAN, THOMAS, born 1710, died 1782. [Abbey St Bathans MI, Berwickshire]

COX, HANNAH, wife of James Cox of Lees, Berwickshire, testament, 1766, C.L. [NRS]

CRAICH, JOHN, a weaver from Peebles, from Leith aboard the Dolphin bound for Darien, 14 July 1698, testament, Edinburgh, 1707. [NRS.CC8.8.83]

The People of the Scottish Borders, 1650-1800

CRAIG, HUGH, son of John Craig a merchant burgess of Edinburgh, minister at Galashiels 1692 until his death in February 1711, husband of Christian Galloway, parents of Hugh, Robert, John, Jean, Francis and Margaret. [F.2.177]

CRAIG, JAMES, a glover in Kelso, a deed, 1715, [NRS.RD3.144.366]

CRAIG, JOHN, son of Hugh Craig minister at Galashiels, a deed, 1715. [NRS.RD4.116.260]

CRAIG, JOHN, born 1763, a vintner in Duns, died 16 February 1805. [Duns MI]

CRAIG, THOMAS, farmer in Auchencraw, testament, 1701, C.L. [NRS]

CRAIK, WILLIAM, in Coldingham, testament, 1753, C.L. [NRS]

CRAMMOND, ELENDER, died 4 January 177-, aged 58. [Mindrum MI]

CRAMOND, MASSIE, in Mertine, spouse to John Clerk, testament, 1675, C.L. [NRS]

CRANSTON, ALEXANDER, in Haliburton, late servant to James Cranston of New Cranston, testament, 1679, C.L. [NRS]

CRANSTON, ANNA, daughter of Alexander Cranston of Moristoun, and spouse to James Pringle of Haltrie, a sasine, 1667. [NRS.RS18.2.19]

CRANSTON, GEORGE, brother of Lord Cranston, a bond, 1758. [NRS.CC18.7.151]

CRANSTOUN, JOHN, minister of Ancrum from 1701, died 7 October 1748. [Ancrum MI, Roxburghshire]

CRANSTOUN, JOHN, a tailor in Coldstream, a sasine, 1768. [NRS.RS18.15.332]

CRANSTOUN, THOMAS, a burgess of Lauder, a sasine, 1678. [NRS.RS18.4.78]

CRANSTON, THOMAS, town clerk of Jedburgh, 1715. [NRS.RD3.145.201]

CRAW, GEORGE, of Netherbyres, a testament, 1705, C.L. [NRS]

CRAW, JOHN, feuar and weaver in Greenlaw, testament, 1780, C.L. [NRS]

CRAWFORD, GEORGE, a candlemaker in Duns, testament, 1736, C.L. [NRS]

The People of the Scottish Borders, 1650-1800

CRAWFORD, WILLIAM, a wright in Duns, testaments, 1686/1688, C.L. [NRS]

CRAWFORD, WILLIAM, a shopkeeper in Kelso, 1785. [NRS.E326.4.1]

CRIGE, WILLIAM, a shopkeeper in Kelso, 1785. [NRS.E326.4.1]

CROMAR, GEORGE, in Coldingham, testament, 1678, C.L. [NRS]

CROMBIE, JOHN, sheriff clerk of Roxburghshire, a deed, 1715. [NRS.RD3.146.447]

CROW, JOHN, in Mervinslaw, a deed, 1757. [NRS.CC18.7.95]

CRYLE, PETER, a mariner, husband of Isabel Steel born 1729, died 18 March 1776. [Lennel MI, Berwickshire]

CULBERTSON, THOMAS, tenant in Traboun, testament, 1748, C.L. [NRS]

CULTON, ANTHONY, born 1745, a laborer from Traquair, Peebles-shire, his wife Janet McCaughter, and children, Marion, Robert, Grizel, Janet, John, and Ann, emigrated via Dumfries aboard the Lovely Nelly to Prince Edward Island in May 1775. [TNA.T47.12]

CUMMING, ALEXANDER, born 1705, died 26 September 1772, Jane Cumming born 1755, died 6 March 1767, and Adam Cumming, born 1745, died 1 September 1772. [Mindrum MI]

CUNNINGHAM, JOHN, of Bogangreen, testaments 1738, C.L. [NRS]

CUNNINGHAM, PATRICK, tenant in Hugh, testament, 1704, C.L. [NRS]

CUNNINGHAM, ROBERT, educated at Edinburgh University 1642, minister at Ashkirk, Selkirkshire, 1649 -1662, 1679, 1689; husband of Mary Elliot. [F.2.168]

CUNNINGHAM, ROBERT, born 1668, son of Patrick Cunningham minister at Kirkton, minister at Wilton, 1694-1712, at Hawick from 1712 until his death on 5 August 1722, husband of Marjory Ker, parents of Robert, Alexander, and Janet. [F.2.114]

CUNNINGHAM, WILLIAM, born 1752, tenant in Blackadder Bank, died 11 January 1817, husband of Margaret Renton, born 1768, died 27 November

The People of the Scottish Borders, 1650-1800

1817, parents of John Cunningham, born 1789, died in Jamaica on 5 October 1809. [Whitsome MI, Berwickshire]

CUPPLES, GEORGE, minister at Swinton, testament, 1799, C.L. [NRS]

CURRER, GEORGE, in Halrule, a deed, 1761. [NRS.CC18.7.379]

CURRER, WILLIAM, in Selkirk, 1783. [NRS.E326.1.210]

CURRIE, ELIZABETH, widow of Alexander Thomson a gardener at Huttonhall, testament, 1737, C.L. [NRS]

CURRIE, PETER, in Duns, testament, 1784, C.L. [NRS]

CURRIE, WILLIAM, smith in Leitholm, testament, 1718, C.L. [NRS]

CURRIE, WILLIAM, skinner in Duns, testament, 1786, C.L. [NRS]

CUTHBERTSON, THOMAS, of Rassriden, father of Joshua, 1678. [NRS,SQR.K17]

CUTHBERTSON, WILLIAM, portioner of Trabroun, testaments, 1757, C.L. [NRS]

DALGLEISH, ALISON, relict of Gavin Melville a merchant in Coldstream, testament, 1751, C.L. [NRS]

DALGLEISH, THOMAS, in Langholm, a deed, 1760. [NRS.CC18.7.295]

DALLAS, ANN and JANE, in Duns, sisters-german to the late Robina Dallas, widow of George Ireland of Drumsay, testament, 1749, C.L. [NRS]

DALLAS, JOHN, bailie of Dallas, testament, 1708, C.L. [NRS]

DALZIEL, GEORGE, in Swinton, testament, 1655, C.L. [NRS]

DARLING, ALEXANDER, a skipper in Eyemouth, a sasine, 1750. [NRS.RS18.13.89]

DARLING, ANDREW, in Bastlerigg, Berwickshire, sasines, 1757-1776. [NRS.RS18.13.517; 16.443/449]

DARLING, DAVID, tenant in Cockburn, testament, 1731, C.L. [NRS]

DARLING, JAMES, feuar in Chirnside, testament, 1715, C.L. [NRS]

The People of the Scottish Borders, 1650-1800

DARLING, JOHN, in Cockburn, sasines, 1696-1706. [NRS.RS18.5.316; 6.18/241; 7.159]

DARLING, PAUL, son of Andrew Darling in Bastlerigg, sasines, 1775-1776. [NRS.RS18.16.443/449]

DARLING, THOMAS, born 1742, died 6 March 1802, his spouse Isabel Ponton, born 1766, died July 1823, son Thomas Darling, born 1797, died in Jamaica on 3 August 1821. [Chirnside MI, Berwickshire]

DARLING, WILLIAM, feuar in Duns, testament, 1699, C.L. [NRS]

DARLING, WILLIAM, a wright in Eyemouth, Berwickshire, sasines, 1769-1776. [NRS.RS18.15.370; 16.450]

DARREN, JAMES, a wright in Hornden, and his spouse Janet Ritchison, a sasine, 1669. [NRS.RS18.2.147]

DARRIE, WILLIAM, in Langbank, testament, 1679, C.L. [NRS]

DAVIDSON, HENRY, born 1687, minister at Galashiels from 1714 until his death on 24 October 1756, husband of Katherine Scott. [F.2.178]

DAVIDSON, JAMES, a shoemaker in Jedburgh, a deed, 1760. [NRS.CC18.7.279]

DAVIDSON, JOHN, born 1665, shepherd to the Earl of Marchmont, died 1732, father of James, born 1708, died 1735. [Polwarth MI, Berwickshire]

DAVIDSON, JOHN, a merchant in Duns, 1785. [NRS.E326.4.1]

DAVIDSON, NICOL, in Birgham, Berwickshire, a sasine, 1762. [NRS.RS18.14.388]

DAVIDSON, PATRICK, saddler and feuar in Duns, a sasine, 1759, testament, 1778, C.L. [NRS.RS18.14.20]

DAVIDSON, ROBERT, a skinner in Kelso, a deed, 1715. [NRS.RD3.145.14]

DAVIDSON, THOMAS, a merchant in Yetholm, a deed, 1760. [NRS.CC18.7.266]

DAVIDSON, THOMAS, born 1728, a surgeon in Kelso, died 15 July 1764, his spouse Jean Scott, born 1730, died 26 August 1794. [Kelso MI]

The People of the Scottish Borders, 1650-1800

DAVIDSON, WILLIAM, a carrier in Jedburgh, deeds, 1758. [NRS.CC18.7.161/178]

DAVIDSON, WILLIAM, a cabinetmaker in Berwick, sasines, 1760-1773. [NRS.RS18.14.215; 15.268; 16.287]

DAVIDSON, WILLIAM, from Peebles-shire, a Captain of the 52nd Regiment of Foot, died in Boston, Massachusetts, probate 1776 PCC.

DAWSON, GEORGE, tenant in Eastfield, testament, 1753, C.L. [NRS]

DAWSON, JAMES, in Smailholm Hospital, a sasine, 1658. [NRS.RS18.4.36]

DAWSON, JAMES, in Harperton, son-in-law of James Thomson a merchant in Kelso, a deed, 1715. [NRS.RD3.144.366]

DAWSON, JAMES, a surgeon in Coldstream, a sasine, 1769. [NRS.RS18.15.352]

DAWSON, JOHN, a gardener at Elbank, testament, 1713, C.L. [NRS]

DAWSON, SAMUEL, tenant in the Mains of Eccles, deeds, 1715. [NRS.RD3.145.810/813]

DEANS, GEORGE, a merchant in Hawick, a deed, 1715. [NRS.RD3.145.497]

DEANS, GEORGE, a butcher in Hawick, a deed, 1759. [NRS.CC18.7.215]

DEANS, MARGARET, spouse of James Speirs a seaman in Eyemouth, Berwickshire, 1722. [NRS.RS18.9.544]

DEAS, JAMES, of Coldingknows, testament, 1719, C.L. [NRS]

DEAS, JOHN, in Lauder, testament, 1690, C.L. [NRS]

DEBEARE, JAMES, a tailor from Berwick, emigrated via London in November 1685. [CLRO/AIA]

DEMPSTER, PETER, a merchant in Longformacus, Berwickshire, and his spouse Jean Muir, a sasine, 1733. [NRS.RS18.11.56]

DENHOLM, DAVID, of Broadmeadows, Berwickshire, a sasine, 1751. [NRS.RS18.13.183]

The People of the Scottish Borders, 1650-1800

DENHOLM, WILLIAM, a merchant in Earlston, a sasine, 1666. [NRS.RS18.1.372]

DENHOLM, WILLIAM, in Earlston, testament, 1684, C.L. [NRS]

DEWAR, DAVID, tailor in West Preston, Berwickshire, a sasine, 1755. [NRS.RS18.13.434]

DEWAR, JOHN, a notary public in Duns, sasines, 1659-1668. [NRS.CS18.1.243/248; 2.75; 4.81]

DEWAR, MATHEW, in Swansfield, testament, 1693, C.L. [NRS]

DEWAR, ROBERT, in West Reston, portioner, sasine, 1755. [NRS.RS18.13.481]

DICK, ADAM, a wright in Earlston, testament, 1728, C.L. [NRS]

DICK, GILBERT, merchant in Paxton, sasines, 1719-1753. [NRS.RS18.9.354; 10.232; 13.304]

DICK, RICHARD, a carpenter who settled in America by 1807, son of George Dick a shoemaker in Jedburgh. [NRS.CS17.1.26/355]

DICK, ROBERT, a merchant in Coldstream, 1785. [NRS.E326/4/1]

DICKINSON, GEORGE, born 1755, died 10 February 1805, his wife Rebecca Ann, born 1769, died 16 October 1809. [Kelso Episcopal MI]

DICKMAN, JOHN, in Cornhill, sasines, 1765. [NRS.RS18.15.91/100]

DICKMAN, WILLIAM, a fisher in Coldstream, sasines, 1765. [NRS.RS18.15.91/99/330]

DICKSON, ADAM, minister at Duns, 1750-1769. [F.2.10]

DICKSON, ALEXANDER, in Longformacus, testament, 1715, C.L. [NRS]

DICKSON, ALEXANDER, a cordiner in Gattonside, a deed, 1715. [NRS.RD4.116.313]

DICKSON, ALEXANDER, son of David Dickson in Hartree, Peebles-shire, a soldier, settled at Houma Chita, West Florida, before 1774. [TNA.CO5.613.257]

DICKSON, ALEXANDER, a shopkeeper in Kelso, 1785. [NRS.E326.4.1]

The People of the Scottish Borders, 1650-1800

DICKSON, ANTHONY, innkeeper in Duns, formerly of Belchester, sasines, 1763-1764. [NRS.RS18.14.469/512]

DICKSON, ARCHIBALD, of Huntlaw, a deed, 1759. [NRS.CC18.7.206]

DICKSON, ARCHIBALD, in Hassendean Burn, a deed, 1760. [NRS.CC18.7.235]

DICKSON, DAVID, of Hartree, Peebles-shire, a former Captain of the 64th Regiment of Foot, was granted 6,000 acres at Houma Chita on the Mississippi River before 1774. [TNA.CO5.613.257]

DICKSON, GEORGE, in Nether Howlaws, testament, 1725, C.L. [NRS]

DICKSON, GEORGE, minister at Bedrule, bonds, 1760. [NRS.CC18.7.244/246]

DICKSON, HECTOR, youngest son of Hector Dickson, a cooper in Peebles, a deed, 1715. [NRS.RD2.105.923]

DICKSON, JAMES, of Belchester, a deed, 1715. [NRS.RD4.116.105]

DICKSON, JAMES, a butcher in Coldstream, Berwickshire, only son of the late Frank Dickson a butcher in Kelso, Roxburghshire, brother of the late Robert Dickson, feuar and butcher in Kelso, versus Catherine, daughter of Thomas Heathers, a weaver in Kelso, alleged wife of the said Robert Dickson and her son Thomas Dickson, 1769. [NRS.CC8.6.965]

DICKSON, JAMES, tenant in Adington, testament, 1769, C.L. [NRS]

DICKSON, JOHN, of Antonshill, testaments, 1740, 1747, 1750, 1752, C.L. [NRS]

DICKSON, JOHN, a shopkeeper in Kelso, 1785. [NRS.E326.4.1]

DICKSON, PETER, a wright and tenant in Berryhaughts, testament, 1781, C.L. [NRS]

DICKSON, ROBERT, born 1763, son of Robert Dickson in Courthill and his wife Janet Bathgate, died in Tobago in 1789. [Nenthorn MI, Berwickshire]

DICKSON, ROBERT, in Kelso, son and heir of Robert Dickson a gardener in Kelso, 1795. [NRS.S/H]

The People of the Scottish Borders, 1650-1800

DICKSON, WILLIAM, son of John Dickson in Whitstead, Glenholm, Peeblesshire, a carpenter, settled in Kingston, Jamaica, before 1765. [NRS.RD2.197.377; RD2.222.203]

DICKSON, Captain WILLIAM, of Ednam, 1784. [NRS.CS228.A.5.27.1]

DOBSON, GEORGE, in Selkirk, 1783. [NRS.E326.1.210]

DODD, JAMES, shipmaster of the Nancy and the Holbeach of Boston, died in Boston, Massachusetts, son of William and Margaret Dodd in Berwisk-on-Tweed, probate 1774 PCC.

DODS, ADAM, in Birgham, sasines, 1754-1764. [NRS.RS18.13.379; 14.397/517]

DODS, ALEXANDER, tenant in Dykethead, testament, 1719, C.L. [NRS]

DODS, GEORGE, in Mellarstain, testament, 1731, C.L. [NRS]

DODS, GEORGE, shoemaker in Birgham, sasines, 1734-1777. [NRS.RS18.11.188; 14.512; 16.362; 17.146]

DODS, JAMES, in Whitchester, a deed, 1760. [NRS.CC18.7.241]

DODS, JAMES, born 1753, tenant in Cherry Trees, died 22 August 1805, his spouse Agnes, born 1738, died 14 August 1823. [Mindrum MI]

DODS, JANET, born 1636, spouse to Walter Scott, died May 1706. [Longnewton MI, Roxburghshire]

DODS, JOHN, sometime tenant in Hardacres, thereafter in Angelraw, testament, 1737, C.L. [NRS]

DODS, JOHN, born 1713, tenant in Maisondieu, died 20 July 1785, his spouse Margaret Swanston, died 16 October 1791. [Kelso MI]

DON, ALEXANDER, of Woodside, eldest son of Patrick Don bailiff of Kelso and brother of Sir Alexander Don of Newton, a deed, 1715. [NRS.RD4.116.1022]

DON, Sir ALEXANDER, of Newton, testament, 1776, C.L. [NRS]

The People of the Scottish Borders, 1650-1800

DON, ANDREW, of Smailholm, son of James Don thereof, brother of Sir Alexander Don of Newton, deeds, 1715. [NRS.RD2.104.986; RD2.105.680; RD3.145.440; RD4.116.129; RD4.116.1022]

DON, Sir JAMES, of Newton, sasine, 1750. [NRS.RS18.13.21]

DONALDSON, ALEXANDER, husband of Agnes Wightman born 1721, died in March 1809, parents of George Donaldson in Jamaica. [Coldstream MI]

DONALDSON, HERCULES, in Birkenside, testament, 1668, C.L. [NRS]

DONALDSON, JOHN, a merchant in Selkirk, a deed, 1715. [NRS.RD3.144.117]

DONALDSON, PETER, mason in Bassenden Muir, sasine, 1776. [NRS.RS18.17.76]

DOUGALL, ANDREW, skipper in Eyemouth, his spouse Isobell Turnbull, and son John Dougall, sasine, 1750. [NRS.RS18.13.93]

DOUGLAS, ALEXANDER, in Spittle, a deed, 1780. [NRS.CC18.7.236]

DOUGLAS, ANDREW, of Ednam House, born 1736, died at Buxton on 11 June 1806. [Kelso Episcopal MI]

DOUGLAS, ARCHIBALD, of Cavers, hereditary sheriff of Roxburghshire, deeds, 1715. [NRS.RD2.104.1025; RD2.105.56/563; RD3.144.330/388; RD2.105.844]

DOUGLAS, ARCHIBALD, of Timperdean, a contract, 1757. [NRS.CC18.7.87]

DOUGLAS, ARCHIBALD, in Spittle, a deed, 1760. [NRS.CC18.7.236]

DOUGLAS, CHRISTOPHER, a physician in Kelso, 1779. [NRS.AD30.1]

DOUGLAS, ELIZABETH, in Spittle, a deed, 1760. [NRS.CC18.7.236]

DOUGLAS, GEORGE, born 1703, a scholar from Linton, Peebles-shire, emigrated via London to Virginia February 1721. [CLRO/AIA]

DOUGLAS, GEORGE, portioner of Hutton, testament, 1743, C.L [NRS]

DOUGLAS, GEORGE, of East Nisbet Miln, sasine, 1757. [NRS.RS18.13.521]

DOUGLAS, HELEN, in Spittle, a deed, 1760. [NRS.CC18.7.236]

The People of the Scottish Borders, 1650-1800

DOUGLAS, HENRY, a surgeon in Selkirk, a deed, 1715. [NRS.RD3.146.463]

DOUGLAS, HUGH, in Swanshiell, a deed, 1758. [NRS.CC18.7.128]

DOUGLAS, ISOBEL, in Spittle, a deed, 1760. [NRS.CC18.7.236]

DOUGLAS, JAMES, born 1641, tenant in Trows, died 7 June 1728; his spouse Esther Riddell, born 1661, died at Slatehills, 23 January 1745. [Cavers MI]

DOUGLAS, JAMES, a merchant in Jedburgh, a deed, 1759. [NRS.CC18.7.229]

DOUGLAS, JAMES, a herd in Muirhouselaw, father of James died 13 September 1793 aged 24, and Janet died 18 March 1795 aged 17. [Longnewton MI, Roxburghshire]

DOUGLAS, JOHN, minister at Jedburgh from 1758 until his death on 16 November 1768, husband of Beatrix Ainslie, parents of Robert, Beatrix, Arabella, and James. [F.2.127]

DOUGLAS, JOHN, of Adderstoun, deeds, 1757/1758. [NRS.CC18.7.87/178]

DOUGLAS, JOHN, in Spittle, a deed, 1760. [NRS.CC18.7.236]

DOUGLAS, JOHN, in Selkirk, 1783. [NRS.E326.1.210]

DOUGLAS, MARGARET, in Spittle, a deed, 1760. [NRS.CC18.7.236]

DOUGLAS, MARY, of Ednam House, born 1752, died in London on 20 February 1807. [Kelso Episcopal MI]

DOUGLAS, ROBERT, born 1716 son of Robert Douglas a merchant in Cumnock, minister at Bunkle from 1765 until his death in 1801, spouse of Christina Margarita Bakker. [F.2.5]

DOUGLAS, ROBERT, in Roughlienookhaugh, a deed, 1760. [NRS.CC18.7.300]

DOUGLAS, ROBERT, born 1720, feuar in Duns, died 18 March 1793, his spouse Isobel Dewar, born 1718, died 1806. [Duns MI, Berwickshire]

DOUGLAS, ROBERT, born 19 July 1747 in Kenmore, minister at Galashiels from 1770 until his death on 15 November 1820, husband of Robina Lothian,

The People of the Scottish Borders, 1650-1800

parents of John, Edward, Helen, Beatrice, Robert, George, and Arabella. [F.2.178]

DOUGLAS, SAMUEL, born 1612, minister at Coldingham 1641-1648, at Eccles 1652, died 1652, husband of Elizabeth Home. [F.2.13]

DOUGLAS, WILLIAM, in Pipertown, testament, 1757, C.L. [NRS]

DOUGLAS, WILLIAM, in Spittle, a deed, 1760. [NRS.CC18.7.236]

DOVE, JAMES, born 1704, smith in Bemerside, died in January 1772, his spouse Margaret Ormiston, born 1729, died March 1791. [Longformacus MI]

DOW, DANIEL, master of the King's boat at Eyemouth, testament, 1769, C.L. [NRS]

DOWNIE, HENRY, in Coldingham sasine, 1773. [NRS.RS18.16.242]

DOWNIE, PATRICK, in Antonshill, sasine, 1773. [NRS.RS18.16.242]

DRUMMOND, GEORGE, son of Rev. Ralph Drummond, minister at Cranshaws from 1785 to 1791. [F.2.7]

DRUMMOND, RALPH, born 1719, minister at Cranshaws from 1762 until his death in 1784, spouse of Jean Trail. [F.2.7]

DRYDEN, GAVIN, born 1731, died 4 April 1813, his spouse Elizabeth Buchan, born 1738, died 12 August 1832. [Cavers MI]

DRYSDALE, ALEXANDER, in Halklaw, sasines, 1732. [NRS.RS18.16.208/210]

DRYSDALE, ALEXANDER, born 1692, tenant in Lennelhill, died 2 May 1755, [Lennel MI, Berwickshire], testament, 1757, C.L. [NRS]; his spouse Isabel Halyburton, born 1700, died 15 March 1756. [Lennel MI]

DRYSDALE, ALEXANDER, born 1728, tenant in Manorhill, died 15 November 1798, his spouse Helen Fergie, born 1734, died 23 September 1811. [Lennel MI, Berwickshire]

DRYSDALE, MARGARET, in Duns, testament, 1718, C.L. [NRS]

The People of the Scottish Borders, 1650-1800

DRYSDALE, ELIZABETH, born 1734, spouse to Thomas Johnston of Templehall, died 13 June 1801. [Ayton MI, Berwickshire]

DUDGEON, ANTONIA, relict of James Dudgeon Quartermaster of the Royal North British Grey Dragoons, testament, 1734, C.L. [NRS]

DUDGEON, THOMAS, a travelling merchant, son of William Dudgeon in Upsettlington, sasine, 1779. [NRS.RS18.17.329]

DUN, JOHN, in Rawburn, testament, 1747, C.L. [NRS]

DUN, JOHN, in Selkirk, a deed, 1757. [NRS.CC18.7.117]

DUN, JOHN, an inn-keeper in Jedburgh, a deed, 1758. [NRS.CC18.7.146]

DUN, THOMAS, in Longformacus, sasines, 1778. [NRS.RS18.17.243/245]

DUNBAR, DAVID, a butcher in Eyemouth, a sasine, 1748. [NRS.RS18.12.446]

DUNBAR, JAMES, minister at Mertoun 1667-1674, minister at Abbey St Bathans, 1675-1681, died 1684 in Edinburgh; husband of {1} Katherine Brodie, parents of Alexander and Mary, [2] Lillias Monro, parents of Lillias. [F.2.2]

DUNBAR, JOHN, a weaver in Coldingham, spouse of Agnes Broun, sasine, 1755. [NRS.RS18.13.428]

DUNBAR, ROBERT, a weaver in Chirnside, testament, 1677, C.L [NRS]

DUNBAR, WILLIAM, of Fulfordlees, a physician in Duns, spouse of Sarah Turnbull, sasines, 1759-1768. [NRS.RS18.14.124; 15.306/345]

DUNLOP, ALISON, relict of Robert Pow a notary in Eyemouth, testament, 1691, C.L. [NRS]

DUNLOP, JAMES, factor to the laird of Moristoun and agent for the Duke of Hamilton, testament, 1721, C.L. [NRS]

DUNLOP, WILLIAM, of Eyemouth, portioner, sasines, 1697. [NRS.RS18.4.52; 5.352]

DUNNET, JOHN, servant to Alexander Haliburton of Coldingknowes, afterwards in Thirlestane, sasines, 1661-1667. [NRS.RS18.2.22; 4.175]

The People of the Scottish Borders, 1650-1800

DUNS, JOHN, portioner of Grueldykes, testament, 1725, C.L. [NRS]

DUNS, JOHN, a glover in Duns, a sasine, 1775. [NRS.RS18.16.410]

DYSART, or SANDILANDS, MATTHEW, born 1704, son of Rev. Matthew Dysart in Coldingham, minister at Eccles from 1731 to his death in 1773, spouse of Jean Hume. [F.2.14]

EASTON, ROBERT, in Greensidehal, a deed, 1762. [NRS.CC18.7.380]

ECKFORD, WILLIAM, tenant in Kelphope, testament, 1765, C.L. [NRS]

EDGAR, ALEXANDER, of Westruther, a deed, 1715. [NRS.RD3.146.264/292]

EDGAR, JAMES, a heritor and surgeon in Duns, died 1765, his spouse Margaret Edgar, died 25 October 1779. [Duns MI, Berwickshire]

EDGAR, RICHARD, of Newton, eldest son of George Edgar of Birgham, parish of Woulstruther, Berwickshire, deeds, 1715. [NRS.RD2.104.560; RD3.146.264/292/318]

EDGAR, THOMAS, son of the late Robert Edgar in Moorton, testament, 1708, C.L. [NRS]

EDGAR, THOMAS, feuar and maltster in Duns, testament, 1757, C.L. [NRS]

EDINGTON, ALEXANDER, born 1730, tenant in Coldingham, died 10 October 1790, his spouse Margaret Muir, born 1745, died 1813. [Coldingham MI]

EDINGTON, JOHN, eldest son of Patrick Edington a feuar in Coldingham, testament, 1700, C.L. [NRS]

EDINGTON, PATRICK, born 1709, farmer in Muirside, died 15 November 1776, husband of Janet Purves, born 1727, died 22 May 1806. [Coldingham MI]

EDINGTON, STEUART, a wright in Duns, testament, 1783, C.L. [NRS]

EDINGTON, ..., born 1670, tenant in Brankston, died 28 March 1747. [Mindrum MI]

EDMISTON, JOHN, born 1723, tenant in Mindrum, died 6 January 1778. [Mindrum MI]

The People of the Scottish Borders, 1650-1800

EDMONDSTON, ALEXANDER, second son of Isobel Don and of Andrew Edmondston of Ednam, a deed, 1715. [NRS.RD4.116.1022]

EDMONSTOUN, DAVID, cooper in Lauder, testament, 1748, C.L. [NRS]

EDMONSTOUN, ISOBEL, relict of William Hog of Harcars, testament, 1734, C.L. [NRS]

EKRON, JAMES, a merchant in Hawick, a deed, 1761. [NRS.CC18.7.761]; a shopkeeper in Hawick, 1785. [NRS.E326.4.1]

ELGIN, GEORGE, from Berwick-on-Tweed, was admitted as a citizen of Rotterdam on 25 July 1754. [Rotterdam Archives]

ELLIOT, ADAM, in Cunziertoun, bonds, 1757/1761. [NRS.CC18.7.90/337]

ELLIOT, ARCHIBALD, in Boonraid, a deed, 1760. [NRS.CC18.7.243]

ELLIOT, ARCHIBALD, in Millsington, deeds, 1756/1757/1758. [NRS.CC18.7.52/66/124/179]

ELLIOT, FRANCIS, a merchant in Hawick, a deed, 1715. [NRS.RD4.116.957]

ELLIOT, GILBERT, tenant in Redcleugh, testament, 1706, C.L. [NRS]

ELLIOT, GILBERT, a bailie of Jedburgh, 1715. [NRS.RD4.116.313]

ELLIOT, Sir GILBERT, of Stobs, a deed of factory, 1758. [NRS.CC18.7.180]

ELLIOT, HENRY, of Harrot, bonds/deeds, 1757/1758. [NRS.CC18.7.58/90/129]

ELLIOT, HENRY, of Peel, a deed, 1757. [NRS.CC18.7.96]

ELLIOT, HENRY, in Flatt, deeds, 1757. [NRS.CC18.7.101/103]

ELLIOT, JOHN, a Covenanter from Teviotdale, was transported from Leith to Jamaica in August 1685, landed at Port Royal, Jamaica. [RPCS.II.329][LJ.44]

ELLIOT, JOHN, a cordiner in Rigg, Teviotdale, a deed, 1715. [NRS.RD4.116.313]

ELLIOT, JOHN, in Clerklands, deeds, 1761/1762. [NRS.CC18.7.378/380/381/384/385]

ELLIOT, JOHN, a merchant in Castleton, a deed, 1759. [NRS.CC18.7.216]

The People of the Scottish Borders, 1650-1800

ELLIOT, KATHARINE, of Midlawmiln, a deed of factory, 1756. [NRS.CC18.7.54]

ELLIOT, ROBERT, a cordiner in Hawick, deeds, 1715. [NRS.RD4.116.169/313]

ELLIOT, ROBERT, from Earlside, Roxburghshire, a thief transported to the colonies in 1726. [NRS.JC12.4]

ELLIOT, ROBERT, of Fennick, a deed, 1757. [NRS.CC18.7.125]

ELLIOT, ROBERT, a tailor in Selkirk, a deed, 1758. [NRS.CC18.7.130]

ELLIOT, THOMAS, a burgess of Selkirk, a deed, 1715. [NRS.RD3.145.895]

ELLIOT, WALTER, of Ormiston, a deed, 1759. [NRS.CC18.7.215]

ELLIOT, WALTER, servant to Robert Wilkie, a herd in Howpasley, a deed, 1760. [NRS.CC18.7.278]

ELLIOT, WILLIAM, a carrier in Minto, a deed, 1715. [NRS.RD2.105.830]

ELLIOT, WILLIAM, of Tarras, a deed, 1757. [NRS.CC18.7.109]

EMELTOUN, CHARLES, a shoemaker in Duns, testament, 1719, C.L. [NRS]

EMERSON, THOMAS, a merchant in Duns, testament, 1704, C.L. [NRS]

ERSKINE, JAMES, of Shielfield, testament, 1702, C.L. [NRS]

ERSKINE, PATRICK, of Shielfield, M.D., a deed, 1757; a sasine, 1778. [NRS.CC18.7.103; RS18.17.261]

EWART, JOHN, a nailer in Foulden, testament, 1684, C.L. [NRS]

FAA, MARY, from Jedburgh, a gypsy transported from Glasgow to Virginia, 1 January 1715. [GR.530]

FAA, PETER, from Jedburgh, a gypsy transported from Glasgow to Virginia, 1 January 1715. [GR.530]

FAILL, WILLIAM, a herd in Hersfields, a deed, 1756. [NRS.CC18.7.23]

FAIR, ISOBEL, in Easter Coldstream, spouse to William Ewart, testament, 1675, C.L. [NRS]

The People of the Scottish Borders, 1650-1800

FAIR, JAMES, born 1750, a weaver in Coldingham, died 11 September 1777. [Coldingham MI, Berwickshire]

FAIR, THOMAS, a merchant in Kelso, 1779. [NRS.AD30/1]

FAIRBAIRN, ARCHIBALD, in Coldstream, testament, 1686, C.L. [NRS]

FAIRBAIRN, GEORGE, a merchant in Kelso, a tack, 1758. [NRS.CC18.7.138]

FAIRBAIRN, JAMES, in Side, a deed, 1757. [NRS.CC18.7.67]

FAIRBAIRN, ROBERT, a miller in St Boswells, deeds, 1759. [NRS.CC18.7.214/218]

FAIRFOUL, ANDREW, minister at Duns from 1652 to 1661. [F.2.9]

FAIRGRIEVE, GEORGE, in Threburnford, Channelkirk, testament, 1671, C.L. [NRS]

FAIRGRIEVE, JOHN, a tailor in Jedburgh, a deed, 1757. [NRS.CC18.7.110]

FAIRLIE, THOMAS, feuar and glover in Duns, testament, 1717, C.L. [NRS]

FALA, JOHN, a shoemaker from Kelso, a Covenanter transported October 1684. [RPCS.9.449]

FALAY, WILLIAM, in Broughtrige, testament, 1683, C.L. [NRS]

FALCONER, ALEXANDER, town clerk of Lauder, testament, 1771, C.L. [NRS]

FALCONER, GEORGE, town clerk of Lauder, testament, 1782, C.L. [NRS]

FALCONER, JOHN, in Peebles, a deed, 1759. [NRS.CC18.7.223]

FALL, JOHN, born 1777 in Roxburghshire, a carpenter who emigrated via London to America, naturalised in New York on 16 June 1825.

FAMILTON, ALISON, spouse of Robert Lidgait in Eccles, testament, 1656, C.L. [NRS]

FELL, ISOBEL, spouse to George Ker in Whinkerstaines, testament, 1653, C.L. [NRS]

The People of the Scottish Borders, 1650-1800

FENWICK, JOHN, from Jedburgh, a gypsy transported from Glasgow to Virginia, 1 January 1715. [GR.530]

FERGIE, PATRICK, in Edrington, and his spouse Jane Cockburn, testament, 1694, C.L. [NRS]

FERGIE, ROBERT, portioner of Paxton, testament, 1681, C.L. [NRS]

FERGUSON, DAVID, sometime in Ugston, Channelkirk, testament, 1781, C.L. [NRS]

FERME, JEAN, relict of William Smith a dyster in Wester Waulkmiln of Cumledge, testament, 1766, C.L. [NRS]

FERRIER, ALEXANDER, of Cowdenknows, and his spouse Jean Deas, testament, 1768, C.L. [NRS]

FERRYLANDS, JEAN, relict of John Cockburn a baxter in Duns, a sasine, 1767. [NRS.RS18.15.244]

FIDDES, WALTER, a wright in Bonjedward, a deed, 1760. [NRS.CC18.7.276]

FISH, JOHN, of Castlelaw, testament, 1737, C.L. [NRS]

FISH, JOHN, a shoemaker in Ayton, spouse of Agnes Dunlop or Darling, a sasine, 1753. [NRS.RS18.13.284]

FISH, RICHARD, mason in Ayton, testament, 1695, C.L. [NRS]

FISHER, ANDREW, heir to his father James Fisher of Beerfalds, second son of the late Andrew Fisher of Westerhousebyres, 1765. [NRS.S/H]

FISHER, CHRISTIAN, in Westerhousebyres, a marriage contract, 1756/1758. [NRS.CC18.7.38/173]

FISHER, ELIZABETH, in Westerhouses, a contract, 1756. [NRS.CC18.7.38]

FISHER, HELEN, relict of John Sheill in Earlston, testament, 1680, C.L. [NRS]

FISHER, JOHN, of Westerhousebyres, a bond, 1757. [NRS.CC18.7.111]

FITTES, AGNES, spouse to Alexander Allanshaw in Foulden, testament, 1672, C.L. [NRS]

The People of the Scottish Borders, 1650-1800

FLEMING, JOHN, weaver in East Reston, testament, 1673, C.L. [NRS]

FLEMING, WILLIAM, born 18 Feb.1729, a physician from Jedburgh, emigrated 1755, settled in Kentucky 1779, died Aug.1795. [VMHB.85.372][WMQ.6.158]

FLETCHER, ANDREW, a herd in Burnfoot, a deed, 1757. [NRS.CC18.7.86]

FLETCHER, JOHN, in Earlston, testament, 1679, C.L. [NRS]

FLINT, WILLIAM, in Ayton, testament, 1668, C.L. [NRS]

FLOCKHART, ALISON, spouse to William Swyne in Hiltoun, testament, 1664, C.L. [NRS]

FOGO, JOHN, tenant in Fishwick, testament, 1728, C.L. [NRS]

FOGO, WILLIAM, in Little Harlaw, testament, 1698, C.L. [NRS]

FOORD, GAWEN, in Leitham Milne Know, testament, 1730, C.L. [NRS]

FOORD, JOHN, minister at Cranshaws from 1655 until his death in 1674, husband of Helen Swinton. [F.2.6]

FOORD, WILLIAM, wright in Jardenfield, testament, 1721, C.L. [NRS]

FORBES, DUNCAN, of Ogstoun, testaments, 1701/1714, C.L. [NRS]

FORESTER, ROBERT, born 1684, a mason in Coldstream, died 4 April 1748, his spouse Isobel Aitchison, born 1683, died 24 July 1747. [Lennel MI, Berwickshire]

FORMAN, CHRISTIAN, widow of Thomas Broun an Excise officer and feuar in Duns, testament, 1800, C.L. [NRS]

FOREMAN, JAMES, in Midburn, a deed, 1757. [NRS.CC18.7.83]

FORMAN, JOHN, a tailor in Hutton, testament, 1743, C.L. [NRS]

FORREST, DAVID, of Gimmersmill, barony of Flemington, parish of Ayton, Berwickshire, a sasine 1758. [LC#3204]

FORREST, PATRICK, a merchant in Eyemouth, testament, 1799, C.L. [NRS]

FORRESTER, ROBERT, in Lochrig, testament, 1698, C.L. [NRS]

FORSON, JOHN, a baxter in Jedburgh, a deed, 1759. [NRS.CC18.7.226]

FORSYTH, BEATRIX, of Newstead, testament, 1713, C.L. [NRS]

FORSYTH, or JAFFREY, ELIZABETH, a meal-dealer in Duns, testament, 1796, C.L. [NRS]

FORSYTH, THOMAS, in Lennelhill, testament, 1711, C.L. [NRS]

FORTUNE, JAMES, in Blacksmill, testament, 1768, C.L. [NRS]

FORTUNE, MARGARET, died 1691, spouse to Robert Drysdale. [Cranshaws MI]

FORTUNE, PATRICK, in Longformacus, testament, 1711, C.L. [NRS]

FORTUNE, WILLIAM, hynd in Redcleughhead, testament, 1764, C.L. [NRS]

FOSTER, ALISON, spouse to Robert Broun a feuar and maltman in Duns, testament, 1674, C.L. [NRS]

FOTHRINGHAM, GRISSELL, in Cockburnspath, testament, C.L. [NRS]

FOULLAR, JANET, in East Gordon, testament, 1655, C.L. [NRS]

FOX, GEORGE, born 1650, son of James Fox in Teviotdale, emigrated via London to Jamaica, January 1685. [CLRO/AIA]

FRAIZER, THOMAS, a shopkeeper in Kelso, 1785. [NRS.E326.4.1]

FRANCE, ALEXANDER, a dyster in Wester Waulkmiln of West Preston, a sasine, 1755. [NRS.RS18.13.425]

FRANCE, MARGARET, in Duns, widow of Christopher Sligh tenant in Buncle, testament, 1790, C.L. [NRS]

FRANK, AGNES, second daughter of the second marriage of the late John Frank of Bughtrig, testament, 1796, C.L [NRS]

FRASER, DANIEL, a wright at Jedburgh Bridge, a deed, 1758. [NRS.CC18.7.173]

FRASER, WALTER, from Falshope, Selkirkshire, settled as a tailor in New York, married Jemima Carter 1784, died in May 1793. [St Andrews Soc.NY.I.203]

The People of the Scottish Borders, 1650-1800

FRATER, JANET, spouse to Thomas Purves in Lidgertwood, testament, 1676, C.L. [NRS]

FREAR, ..., a hatter from Berwick, a Quaker, died in Edinburgh, 1700. [NRS.Scottish Quaker Records, E.11.7]

FRENCH, ELSPETH, relict of James Gordon of Gordonbank, testament, 1754, C.L. [NRS]

FRENCH, JOHN, bailie of Darnchester, testaments, 1727/1736/1743, C.L. [NRS]

FRENCH, ROBERT, a baxter in Eyemouth, and his spouse Sophia Kerr, a sasine, 1755. [NRS.RS18.13.424]

FRIER, JAMES, son of Archibald Frier, a weaver in Gattonside, a sasine, 1695. [NRS.RS18.5.285]

FRIER, JOHN, in Melrose, a deed, 1758. [NRS.CC18.7.141]

FRISKEN, JAMES, portioner of Hutton and tenant of Wester Ointonan, testament, 1772, C.L. [NRS]

FUIRD, JOHN, minister at Chrinshaws, testament, 1675, C.L. [NRS]

FULLARTON, JOHN, a wright in East Gordon, testament, 1744, C.L. [NRS]

FULTON, ADAM, feuar in Coldingham, a sasine, 1755. [NRS.RS18.13.450]

FULTON, ELSPETH, spouse to James Grierson portioner of Coldingham, testament, 1727, C.L. [NRS]

FULTON, GEORGE, from Coldingham, Berwickshire, a member of the Scots Charitable Society of Boston 1762. [NEHGS]

FULTON, MARK, son of Alexander Fulton, portioner of Coldingham, a sasine, 1753. [NRS.RS18.13.300]

FULTON, MARK, born 1720, tenant in Bessborough West Mains, died 10 July 1801. [Coldingham MI, Berwickshire]

FULTON, ROBERT, son of Adam Fulton, a maltman in Coldingham, a sasine, 1728. [NRS.RS18.10.244]

The People of the Scottish Borders, 1650-1800

GALBRAITH, WILLIAM, minister at Bothkennar 1654-1662, at Chirnside 1662-1668, at Morebattle 1668-1682, at Jedburgh 1682- 1689, husband of Dorothea Kerr, a widow. [F.2.126]

GARDINER, WILLIAM, born 1750, a weaver in Duns, died 3 April 1787, his spouse Margaret Weatherhead, born 1749, died 7 August 1813. [Duns MI]

GAVIN, DAVID, of Langton, testaments, 1773/1775. C.L. [NRS]

GIB, GEORGE, in Home, testament, 1711. C.L. [NRS]

GIBSON, GEORGE, a tailor and feuar in Duns, testament, 1759. C.L. [NRS]

GIBSON, JAMES, tenant in Hornden, testament, C.L. [NRS]

GIBSON, JOHN, tenant in West Gordon and his children William, John, Andrew, James and Marion, testament, 1728. C.L. [NRS]

GIBSON, WILLIAM, a laborer in Fogo, testament, 1743. C.L. [NRS]

GIGIE, ELIZABETH, in Harlow, near Eccles, testament, 1785. C.L. [NRS]

GILCHRIST, AGNES, in Whitsom, testament, 1677. C.L. [NRS]

GILCHRIST, MARGARET, spouse of George Currie a merchant in Duns, a sasine, 1661. [NRS.RS18.4.182]

GILCHRIST, ROBERT, son of John Gilchrist in Duns, Berwickshire, a merchant who emigrated from Ayr to Barbados, died there in 1649, testament, 1653, Edinburgh. [NRS.CC8.8.67]

GILES, ROBERT, in Leitbrae, testament, 1671. C.L. [NRS]

GILKIE, ALEXANDER, son of James Gilkie a mason in Langtoun, a sasine, 1679. [NRS.RS18.4.124]

GILLAN, ROBERT, born 7 June 1761, son of Robert Gillan minister at Lessudden, minister at Ettrick 1787-1789, at Hawick 1789-1800, died 7 May 1824, husband of Marion Campbell, parents of Robert, William, Margaret, Joseph, Alexander, Cauvin, and Agnes. [F.2.115]

GILLILAND, JAMES, minister at Greenlaw, testament, 1725. C.L. [NRS]

The People of the Scottish Borders, 1650-1800

GIRDWOOD, ISOBEL, spouse to William Bookless in Grinlaw, testament, 1675. C.L. [NRS]

GLADSTANES, ABRAHAM, heir to his grandfather Walter Gladstanes of Dod, 1676. [NRS.S/H]

GLADSTAINS, JAMES, in Chapelhill, deeds, 1757-1761. [NRS.CC18.7.86/116/118/178/242/243/381]

GLADSTAINS, JOHN, in Chapelhill, a deed, 1757. [NRS.CC18.7.61]

GLADSTAINS, JOHN, in Mabenlaw, a deed, 1758. [NRS.CC18.7.178]

GLADSTAINS, JOHN, in Whitelaws, a deed, 1760. [NRS.CC18.7.243]

GLADSTAINS, JOHN, a writer in Hawick, deeds, 1757-1759. [NRS.CC18.7.110/225/226]

GLADSTAINS, ROBERT, in Hardenburnfoot, deeds, 1757. [NRS.CC18.7.115/116]

GLADSTAINS, WILLIAM, in Branxholm, deeds, 1757-1758. [NRS.CC18.7.115/178]

GLADSTAINS, WILLIAM, a merchant in Duns, 1785. [NRS.E326.4.1]

GLEN, ALEXANDER, minister at Kirkton, at Galashiels 1757-1769, a deed, 1758. [NRS.CC18.7.129][F.2.178]

GLENDINNING, JACOB, in Newton of Coldstream, sasines, 1753/1769. [NRS.RS18..13/321; 15/402]

GLENDINNING, SIMON, in Coldstream, sasines, 1768-1770. [NRS.RS18.15/339/471]

GLOWHOLME, ANDREW, in Hutton, testament, 1753. C.L. [NRS]

GOATHRA, BESSIE, in Prendergaist, spouse to William Burgan, testament, 1682. C.L. [NRS]

GOODLAD, GEORGE, in Swinton, testament, 1675. C.L. [NRS]

GORDON, ALEXANDER, of Earlston, Berwickshire, born 1650, a Covenanter refugee in Holland from 1679, died 1726. [NRS.NA.24245]

The People of the Scottish Borders, 1650-1800

GORDON, ALEXANDER, born 7 April 1733, an innkeeper in Duns, died 1 May 1805, his spouse Jean Cowlie, born 1738, died 4 April 1813. [Duns MI]

GORDON, CHARLES, from Aberdeenshire, educated at Aberdeen University, minister of Veere in Zealand from 1686 to 1691, minister at Ashkirk, Selkirkshire, from 1695 until his death on 19 April 1710; husband of Rosina Campbell, parents of George, James, and Christian. [F.2.169]

GORDON, ELIZABETH, daughter of .....Gordon and his wife Janet Law in Maxwellheugh, died 1667. [NRS.SQR.K11]

GORDON, FRANCIS, son of Sir Robert Gordon of Earlston, a merchant, settled in Yecomico, Va., before 1759, testament, 23 Apr.1770, Comm. Edinburgh. [NRS.CC8.8.121; CS16.1.103]

GORDON, GEORGE, son of Rev. Charles Gordon in Ashbank, Roxburghshire, a merchant and planter in Md., dead by 1748. [APB.3.139]

GORDON, GEORGE, of Gordonbank, testament, 1784. C.L. [NRS]

GORDON, THOMAS, advocate, son and heir of the late Thomas Gordon a Writer to the Signet, at Carrsfield, testament, 1759. C.L. [NRS]

GOTTERSON, WILLIAM, in Mellarstaines, testament, 1669. C.L. [NRS]

GOURIE, ALISON, in Foulden, testament, 1679. C.L. [NRS]

GOURLAY, JOHN, in Duns, a sasine, 1670. [NRS.RS18.2.247]

GOURNS, DANIEL, in Ulston, a deed, 1756. [NRS.CC18.7.21]

GOVAN, WILLIAM, of Hermistone, heir to his uncle William Govan of Hermistone who died on 25 January 1795, 1796. [NRS.S/H]

GOWDELOCK, GEORGE, a merchant in Legertwood, testament, 1767. C.L. [NRS]

GOWDIE, JOHN, minister at Earlston, testament, 1778. C.L. [NRS]

GRADEN, ROBERT, son of Alexander Graden, a mason in Coldstream, sasine, 1710. [NRS.RS18.8.116]

The People of the Scottish Borders, 1650-1800

GRAHAME, JAMES, in Falnash, a deed, 1757. [NRS.CC18.7.58]

GRAHAM, ROBERT, feuar in Coldingham, and his spouse Christian Weild, testament, 1762. C.L. [NRS]

GRAHAM, THOMAS, from Skirling, Peebles-shire, a Covenanter, transported from Leith to East New Jersey aboard the Henry and Francis in September 1685. [RPCS.II.173]

GRANT, ALEXANDER, from Berwickshire, a merchant in Jamaica later in London, 1773. [NRS.RS18.16.228]

GRANT, ANDREW, from Berwickshire, a merchant in Jamaica later in London, 1774. [NRS.RS18.16.317]

GRANT, WALTER, born 1707, a barber from Teviotdale, a Jacobite, transported via London to Jamaica 20 March 1747, landed in Jamaica 1747. [P.2.264][TNA.CO137.58]

GRANT, WILLIAM, born 1728, a mason and feuar in Duns, died 30 July 1788, his spouse Jean Scott, born 1730, died 27 May 1808. [Duns MI, Berwickshire]

GRAY, ADAM, tenant in Clockmiln, testament, 1723. C.L. [NRS]

GRAY, GEORGE, portioner of Nether Ancrum and Ashieburn, a tack, 1756. [NRS.CC18.7.24]

GRAY, JAMES, minister at Kelso 1687-1689. [F.2.71]

GRAY, JOHN, keeper of the Register of Sasines of Berwickshire, testament, 1736. C.L. [NRS]

GRAY, JOHN, a shopkeeper in Kelso, 1785. [NRS.E326.4.1]

GRAY, THOMAS, feuar in Newtoun of Coldstream, testament, 1754. C.L. [NRS]

GRAY, WILLIAM, parson of Duns from 1666 until 1689, [F.2.9]; testament, 1714. C.L. [NRS]

GRAY, WILLIAM, miller in Overtonmiln, deeds, 1757. [NRS.CC18.7.69/102]

GRAY, WILLIAM, a skinner in Kelso, a deed, 1758. [NRS.CC18.7.150]

The People of the Scottish Borders, 1650-1800

GRAYDEN, GRACE, only child of the late John Grayden H.M. servant, spouse to James Douglas of Earnslaw, testament, 1698. C.L. [NRS]

GREENFIELD, MARGARET, of Whitsom, spouse to George Auld, testament, 1676. C.L. [NRS]

GREENLAW, ROBERT, in Foulden, testament, 1653. C.L. [NRS]

GREENLAW, WILLIAM, servant to James Wilson tenant in Foulden Dean, testament, 1759. C.L. [NRS]

GREIG, MARY, from Duns, Berwickshire, a cattle-thief, transported September 1768. [AJ.1079]

GRIERSON, ROBERT, shoemaker in Coldingham, testament, 1705. C.L. [NRS]

GRIEVE, ALEXANDER, a merchant in Greenlaw, testament, 1795. C.L. [NRS]

GRIEVE, JAMES, in Todshawhaugh, a bond, 1758. [NRS.CC18.7.144]

GRIEVE, JAMES, a merchant in Hopeshaws, a deed, 1756. [NRS.CC18.7.45]

GRIEVE, PATRICK, a merchant in Eyemouth, testament, 1769. C.L. [NRS]

GRIEVE, WALTER, from Jedburgh, Roxburghshire, a thief transported to the colonies in May 1726. [NRS.JC27.12.4]

GRIEVE, WILLIAM, junior, a vintner in Duns, testaments, 1756/1758. C.L. [NRS]

GROSSET, or MUIRHEAD, JAMES, of Breadisholm, Berwickshire, a merchant in Lisbon, 1766. [NRS.RS18.15.220]

GULLAN, WILLIAM, minister at Ladykirk, testaments, 1697/1699. C.L. [NRS]

GUTHRIE, ROBERT, in Selkirk, 1783. [NRS.E326.1.210]

HAIG, ANDREW, in Bemersyde, Berwickshire, a Quaker, circa 1670, father of David and Hannah. [NRS.Scottish Quaker Records, 17.86/87]

HAIG, ANDREW, in Netherstanes, died 1694, his widow Margaret Dods, died 1699. [NRS.SQR.K.17]

HAIG, ANTHONY, of Bemerside, a deed, 1715. [NRS.RD2.104.1065]

The People of the Scottish Borders, 1650-1800

HAIG, DAVID, of Bemersyde, testament, 1673. C.L. [NRS]

HAIG, DAVID, born 1667, died 4 July 1752, his spouse Agnes Scruvin, born 1668, died 26 October 1754. [Dryburgh Abbey MI, Berwickshire]

HAIG, EMANUEL, second son of the late Anthony Haig of Bemersyde, testament, 1735. C.L. [NRS]

HAIG, JAMES, of Bemerside, eldest son of James Haig of Bemerside, heir to his second cousin Isaac Haig of Third, 1794. [NRS.S/H]

HAIG, WILLIAM, born 28 March 1646, second son of David Haig of Bemersyde, Berwickshire, married Mary, daughter of Gavin Lawrie in London 1673, Receiver General of West New Jersey, 1685, died 29 July 1688 in Burlington, West New Jersey, a Quaker. ['Haigs of Bemersyde', Edinburgh, 1881, p.44] [NRS.RD2.82.418][NYGHR.XXX][NJSA.Liber A]

HAIG, WILLIAM, born 20 June 1670, son of Anthony Haig of Bemersyde, a merchant in Antigua. ['Haigs of Bemersyde', Edinburgh, 1881, p.443]

HAIR, JAMES, in Jedburgh, a deed, 1756. [NRS.CC18.7.54]

HAITLIE, ROBERT, in East Mains of Wedderburn, testament, 1731. C.L. [NRS]

HAITLIE, WILLIAM, tenant in Blackadder Mains, testament, 1729. C.L. [NRS]

HAITLIE, WILLIAM, tenant in Blackadder Mains, testament, 1758. C.L. [NRS]

HALDANE, JAMES, a merchant in Jedburgh, Roxburghshire, a thief transported from Glasgow to New England in June 1722. [NRS.JC12.3]

HALIDAY, THOMAS, in Swinton Milne, testament, 1684. C.L. [NRS]

HALIWELL, JANET, spouse to James Wilson in Dalcove, testament, 1668. C.L. [NRS]

HALIWELL, THOMAS, in Longhaugh, a deed, 1756. [NRS.CC18.7.28]

HALL, ELIZABETH, daughter to the late John Hall in West Restoun, testament, 1721. C.L. [NRS]

HALL, GEORGE, born 1780 in Roxburghshire, a merchant in Charleston, South Carolina, naturalised there 15 June 1812. [NARA.M1183/1]

HALL, HENRY, of Haughhead, a deed, 1757. [NRS.CC18.7.99]

HALL, JAMES, minister of Abbey St Bathans from 1719 to his death in 1754, husband of Margaret Johnston, parents of John, George, Janet, Margaret, James, Jean, and Marion. [F.2.2]

HALL, JAMES, a physician in Duns, testament, 1797. C.L. [NRS]

HALL, JOHN, in Houston, a deed, 1760. [NRS.CC18.7.304]

HALL, JOHN, born 1767, died 2 April 1843, husband of Isabella Grieve, born 1780, died in Wisconsin 13 January 1860. [Coldingham MI, Berwickshire]

HALL, JOHN, in Ulston, a deed, 1756. [NRS.CC18.7.21]

HALL, JOHN, a dyer in Newbigging, a deed, 1756. [NRS.CC18.7.27]

HALL, MARGARET, died 12 February 1698. [Mindrum MI]

HALL, ROBERT, died 12 February 1698. [Mindrum MI]

HALL, ROBERT, born 1753, shepherd at Shotton, died at Marden 9 December 1816, his wife Margaret, born 1771, died 2 June 1795. [Mindrum MI]

HALL, WALTER, born 1727, died 10 June 1759, his spouse Agnes born 1715, died 15 October 1790, and their daughter Jane, born 1750, died 12 April 1782. [Mindrum MI]

HALL, WILLIAM, of Whitshall, one of the Principal Clerks of Session, testament, 1749. C.L.[NRS]

HALL, WILLIAM, a merchant in Berwick, a deed, 1757. [NRS.CC18.7.119]

HALLIBURTON, JAMES, in Mertine, testament, 1675. C.L. [NRS]

HALLIBURTON, MARGARET, relict of Andrew Greenfield in Merton, testament, 1670. C.L. [NRS]

HALLIBURTON, SIMON, of Howcleuch and Borthwickmains, born 5 May 1720, second son of John Halliburton, MD in Jedburgh, and his wife Christian Elliot,

The People of the Scottish Borders, 1650-1800

educated at Edinburgh University, minister at Ashkirk from 1763 until his death on 28 April 1797; husband of Elizabeth Elliot, parents of Katherine, John, Robert, and Thomas. [F.2.170]

HAMILTON, GEORGE, a dyster in Gramslaw, a deed, 1757. [NRS.CC18.7.62]

HAMILTON, HENDRY, in Stitchill, 1684, his wife Janet Mason, died 1694, his sister? Marion Hamilton, in Stitchill, 1684, died 1703, Quakers. [RPCS.3.IX.680] [NRS.SQR,K17]

HAMILTON, WILLIAM, schoolmaster of Duns, testament, 1697. C.L. [NRS]

HANDISYDE, JOHN, in Thirlstaine, testament, 1665. C.L. [NRS]

HANDISYDE, WILLIAM, a merchant in Kelso, a deed, 1715. [NRS.RD2.105.669]

HANGITSYDE, JAMES, in Coldstream, testament, 1654. C.L. [NRS]

HANNA, WILLIAM, a Covenanter from the Borders, transported from Leith to East New Jersey aboard the Henry and Francis 5 September 1685. [RPCS.II.94]

HAPPER, THOMAS, portioner of Coldingham, testament, 1697. C.L. [NRS]

HARDIE, JOHN, born around 1632, from Gordon, Berwickshire, a minister in exile in Leiden and Rotterdam from 1683 to 1687. [SEC]

HARDY, JOHN, a merchant in Hawick, a deed, 1761. [NRS.CC18.7.320]

HARDY, THOMAS, in Lauder, testaments, 1781-1789. C.L. [NRS]

HARDY, WILLIAM, a flesher in Hawick, 1758. [NRS.CC18.7.147]

HARDIE, WILLIAM, born 1709, schoolmaster in Polwarth, died 7 November 1783, his spouse Margaret Wilson, born 1710, died 23 July 1793. [Polwarth MI]

HARDY, JAMES, a shopkeeper in Kelso, 1785. [NRS.E326.4.1]

HARDY, ..., deacon of the cordiners in Kelso, 1715. [NRS.RD4.116.313]

HARE, BETTY, in Stonedge, a bond, 1758. [NRS.CC18.7.183]

HARPER, GEORGE, in Grueldykes, testament, 1670. C.L. [NRS]

HART, JAMES, a smith in Midlam, a deed, 1758. [NRS.CC18.7.145]

The People of the Scottish Borders, 1650-1800

HART, WALTER, son of James Hart provost of Edinburgh, minister at Bunkle 1706 to his death in 1761, husband of (1) Ann Daes (2) Sarah Kerr. [F.2.5]

HARTLIE, JOHN, in Spences Mains, testament, 1683. C.L. [NRS]

HASTIE, JAMES, in Lamerton, testament, 1678. C.L. [NRS]

HASTIE, WILLIAM, a messenger in Duns, testament, 1692. C.L. [NRS]

HASWELL, ADAM, portioner of Ulston, a deed, 1759. [NRS.CC18.7.210]

HASWELL, JAMES, merchant in Jedburgh, son of the late James Haswell in Prouston, heir to his aunt Isabella Haswell, late spouse of William Elliot a bailie of Jedburgh, 1702. [NRS.S/H]

HAVIE, HELEN, in Ladykirk, testament, 1655. C.L. [NRS]

HAY, ELIZABETH, widow of Abraham Home minister at Whittingham, testament, 1790. C.L. [NRS]

HAY, GEORGE, a shopkeeper in Kelso, 1785. [NRS.E326.4.1]

HAY, or BRIGGS, JEAN, in Hawick, a deed, 1757. [NRS.CC18.7.105]

HAY, ROBERT, born 1718, a feuar in Kelso, died 4 October 1775, his spouse Agnes Brown, born 1715, died 20 March 1788. [Kelso MI]

HAY, WILLIAM, a gardener from East Gordon, Berwickshire, emigrated via London to Maryland in February 1754. [CLRO/AIA]

HAY, WILLIAM, a wright in Chirnside, testament, 1782. C.L. [NRS]

HEATHERSGILL, ROBERT, from Jedburgh, transported from Leith to Barbados, 17 April 1666. [ETR.106]

HEGGART, ROBERT, an apprentice coppersmith in Kelso, a deed, 1761. [NRS.CC18.7.337]

HEIDSHOIP, ANTHONY, from Jedburgh, transported from Leith to Barbados, 17 April 1666. [Edinburgh Tolbooth Register.106]

HELM, HENRY, portioner of Midlem, a deed, 1761. [NRS.CC18.7.342]

The People of the Scottish Borders, 1650-1800

HELM, JOHN, portioner of Midlem, a deed, 1761. [NRS.CC18.7.342]

HELM, WILLIAM, an innkeeper in Midlem, deeds, 1756. [NRS.CC18.7.13/20]

HENDERSON, ADAM, a flesher in Kelso, deeds, 1758-1761; 1770. [NRS.CC18.7.137/307/321/368; CS228.A.3.48]

HENDERSON, AGNES, relict of Robert Lindsay tenant in Mellarstaines, testament, 1722. C.L. [NRS]

HENDERSON, ARCHIBALD, in Halnash, a deed, 1758. [NRS.CC18.7.179]

HENDERSON, ARCHIBALD, a herd in Unthank, a deed, 1757. [NRS.CC18.7.60]

HENDERSON, GEORGE, a herd in Overwood, testament, 1740. C.L. [NRS]

HENDERSON, JAMES, born 1750, feuar in Ayton, died 10 November 1829, husband of Jean Tait, born 1753, died 22 September 1830, parents of Hume Henderson, born 1784, died in Jamaica on 14 December 1807. [Coldingham MI, Berwickshire]

HENDERSON, JAMES, a fisher in Newton of Coldstream, sasine, 1777. [NRS.RS18.17.153]

HENDERSON, JANET, relict of Andrew Currie a burgess of Lauder, testament, 1757. C.L. [NRS]

HENDERSON, JOHN, of Kirktonhill, M.D., sasine, 1755. [NRS.RS18.13.461]

HENDERSON, JOHN, in Berrysfell, a deed, 1756. [NRS.CC18.7.23]

HENDERSON, JOHN, in Selkirk, 1783. [NRS.E326.1.210]

HENDERSON, MARK, town clerk of Lauder, sasine, 1714. [NRS.RS18.8.547]

HENDERSON, RICHARD, fisher in Newton of Coldstream, sasine, 1777. [NRS.RS18..17.153]

HENDERSON, ROBERT, of Todrig, testament, 1728. C.L. [NRS]

HENDERSON, THOMAS, died 1722. [Cavers MI]

HENDERSON, THOMAS, a burgess of Lauder, and his wife Janet, testament, 1755. C.L. [NRS]

HENDERSON, THOMAS, in Sintounheugh, a deed, 1761. [NRS.CC18.7.344]

HENDERSON, THOMAS, a flesher in Jedburgh, a deed, 1758. [NRS.CC18.7.137]

HENDERSON, WALTER, a merchant in Kelso, a deed, 1761. [NRS.CC18.7.368]

HENDERSON, WILLIAM, a smith in Denholm, a deed, 1760. [NRS.CC18.7.292]

HENRICKS, JANE, in Eyemouth, testament, 1795. C.L. [NRS]

HEPBURN, EUPHAM, daughter of Patrick Hepburn of Nunraw, and spouse of George Home of St Bathans, sasine, 1692. [NRS.RS18.5.203]

HEPBURN, JAMES, son of James Hepburn of Humby, sasine, 1774. [NRS.RS18.16.365]

HEPBURNE, ROBERT, Sheriff-clerk of Berwick, testament, 1672. C.L. [NRS]

HERIOTT, ALEXANDER, servant in Prentown, testament, 1673. C.L. [NRS]

HERIOT, FRANCIS, son of Robert Heriot, a barber and wigmaker in Eyemouth, sasines, 1750, 1762, 1764. [NRS.RS18.13.6; 14.410; 15.45]

HERIOT, JAMES, a weaver in Duns, sasine, 1748. [NRS.RS18.12.404]

HERMISTON, MARION, in Fogo, testament, 1690. C.L. [NRS]

HEWAT, ALEXANDER, minister at Edram, testament, 1678. C.L. [NRS]

HEWAT, JAMES, born 25 January 1736, tenant of Flasswoodsheads and Redhall, died 1 March 1801. [Westruther MI, Berwickshire]

HEWIT, JAMES, born 1733, died 19 February 1793. [Ayton MI]

HILL, JAMES, born 1719, feuar in Ayton, died 7 July 1781, his spouse Ann Keay, born 1720, died 7 January 1771, their daughter Jane born 1746, died 5 February 1816. [Ayton MI, Berwickshire]

HILL, JAMES, born 1752, a mason in Ayton, died 10 October 1778. [Ayton MI, Berwickshire]]

The People of the Scottish Borders, 1650-1800

HILLS, JAMES, born 1787 in Berwickshire, settled as a merchant in Savanna, Georgia, 1804, died 17 July 1829. [Georgia Republican, 20.8.1829]

HILL, JOHN, a weaver in Duns, sasines, 1678-1693. [NRS.RS18.4.101/102; 5.245]

HILL, THOMAS, a weaver in Duns, testament, 1664. C.L. [NRS]

HILL, WILLIAM, a skipper in Eyemouth, testament, 1762. C.L. [NRS]

HILLSON, GEORGE, in Ord, Berwick, later in Gainslaw Loan House, sasines, 1771, 1778. [NRS.RS18.16.56; 17.226]

HILLSON, JEAN, in Bassindean, testament, 1655. C.L. [NRS]

HILLSON, THOMAS, born 1748, a shoemaker in Kelso, died 5 March 1815, his wife Barbara Taylor, born 1749, died 3 August 1816. [Kelso MI]

HISLOP, ANDREW, a smith in Earlston, sasines, 1757, 1759. [NRS.RS18.13.534; 14.37]

HISLOP, JAMES, a baxter burgess of Lauder, testament, 1758. C.L. [NRS]

HISLOP, JANET, relict of Andrew Dickson miller at Lady's Miln in Lauder, testament, 1732. C.L. [NRS]

HISLOP, ROBERT, a weaver in Whitsome, sasine, 1743. [NRS.RS18.12.3]

HOBKIRK, ANDREW, in Harrot, a deed, 1759. [NRS.CC18.7.215]

HOBKIRK, WALTER, in Mabonlaw, a deed, 1760. [NRS.CC18.7.298]

HODGE, JOHN, in Coldingham, a sasine, 1700; testament, 1701. C.L. [NRS.RS18.6.112]

HOGARTH, ADAM, in Duns, sasine, 1696. [NRS.RS18.5.325]

HOGARTH, ANDREW, born 1749, shepherd in Shildean, died 27 October 1810, husband of June. [Mindrum MI]

HOGG, ADAM, in Pearslaw, a deed, 1761. [NRS.CC18.7.343]

HOGG, ALEXANDER, tenant in Pyetshaw, testament, 1759. C.L. [NRS]

The People of the Scottish Borders, 1650-1800

HOGG, ALEXANDER, a merchant in Eyemouth, testament, 1795. C.L. [NRS]

HOGG, CHRISTIAN, spouse of Daniel Dow a Customs officer in Eyemouth, a sasine, 1754. [NRS.RS18.13.355]

HOGG, JOHN, a hind in Handixwood, testament, 1719. C.L. [NRS]

HOGG, ROBERT, merchant in Coldstream, 1713. [NRS.RS18.8.381]

HOGG, Sir ROGER, of Harcarse, testament, 1704. C.L. [NRS]

HOGG, THOMAS, in Eckford, a deed, 1758. [NRS.CC18.7.165]

HOGG, WILLIAM, portioner of Dryburgh, sasine, 1672. [NRS.RS18.3.36]

HOGGART, GEORGE, tenant in Byrewalls, testament, 1738. C.L. [NRS]

HOGGART, WILLIAM, in Gordon Milne, testament, 1682. C.L. [NRS]

HOLIWELL, ARTHUR, in Dalcove and Manerhill, sasines, 1686. [NRS.RS4.478/479]

HOLSON, HUGH, in Netherraw, a deed, 1757. [NRS.CC18.7.57]

HOME, ABRAHAM, of Kennetside-head, testament, 1723. C.L. [NRS]

HOME, Sir ALEXANDER, of Renton, testaments, 1698/1699/1705. C.L. [NRS]

HOME, ALEXANDER, of Ayton, deeds, 1715. [NRS.RD3.144.500; RD3.146.566]

HOME, ALEXANDER, from Berwickshire, in St Kitts, 1769. [NRS.RS18.15.371]

HOME, Sir ANDREW, of Kimmerghame, testaments, 1730/1731. C.L. [NRS]

HOME, FRANCIS, from Wedderburn, Duns, Berwickshire, a Jacobite transported from Liverpool aboard the Elizabeth and Anne on 29 June 1716, landed in Virginia. [SPC.1716.310][CTB.31.208][VSP.1.185]

HOME, Sir GEORGE, from Eccles, Berwickshire, settled at Port Royal, Nova Scotia, in 1630. [RPCS.3.543]

HOME, GEORGE, minister at Abbey St Bathans, 1699 to his death in 1705, husband of Jean Hamilton, parents of Ninian. [F.2.2]

The People of the Scottish Borders, 1650-1800

HOME, GEORGE, minister at Selkirk 1694-1699, thenat Abbey St Bathans from until his death in 1718, husband of Rebecca Pow, parents of John, Sophia and Jane, [F.2.195/2]; testament, 1718. C.L. [NRS]

HOME, GEORGE, born 1698 in Wedderburn, Duns, Berwickshire, a surveyor, a Jacobite transported in 1721, settled in Culpepper County, Virginia, married Elizabeth Proctor, died 1760. [OT.91]

HOME, GEORGE, born 1717, son of George Home of Whitefield, Duns, Berwickshire, a writer in Edinburgh, a Jacobite transported aboard the Veteran from Liverpool on 5 May 1747 to the Leeward Islands, landed in Martinique in June 1747. [P.2.290][TNA.SP36.102]

HOME, HENRY, portioner of Coldingham, testament, 1737. C.L. [NRS]

HOME, NINIAN, of Billie, testaments, 1749/1755. C.L. [NRS]

HOME, NINIAN, of Paxton, Berwickshire, who settled in Grenada and returned before 1766. [NRS.RS18.15.227; 16.301; 17.80/171/297/378/379/381/384]

HOME, WILLIAM, born 1686 in Greenlaw, minister at Fogo from 1722 until his death in 1756, spouse of Isabella Oliphant. [F.2.16]

HOME, WILLIAM, born 1710, minister at Fogo from 1758 until his death in 1784, spouse of Mary Roddam, parents of, inter alia, Walter Home, Colonel of the 42nd Regiment who fought throughout the American War of Independence. [F.2.16]

HOOD, ANDREW, wright in Coldstream, sasine, 1764. [NRS.RS18.15.7]

HOOD, JAMES, born 1714, a wright in Dryburgh, died 1799, his spouse Isabel Spotswood, born 1718, died 1809. [Dryburgh Abbey MI, Berwickshire]

HOOD, JOHN, tenant in West Nisbet, testament, 1735. C.L. [NRS]

HOOPER, WILLIAM, a minister from Ednam, Roxburghshire, emigrated 7 July 1747 to New England, settled in Boston, Massachusetts, died 14 April 1767. [EMA.34][SO.107]

HOPE, JOHN, from Galashiels, Selkirkshire, a member of the Scots Charitable Society of Boston, 1819. [NEHGS]

HOPE, ROBERT, born 1754, a servant in Roxburghshire, a thief transported in May 1771. [NRS.RH2.4.255]

HOPKIRK, GEORGE, born 1765, son of Alexander Hopkirk and his wife Jean Briggs, died at Roxburgh Castle, Jamaica, 11 March 1813. [Dryburgh Abbey MI, Berwickshire]

HOPPER, JOHN, maltman in Coldingham, sasine, 1755. [NRS.RS13.436]

HOPPER, ROBERT, in Kelso, sasine, 1772. [NRS.RS18.16.153]

HOPPER, THOMAS, a feuar in Coldingham, sasine, 1757. [NRS.RS18.13.519]

HOPRINGLE, JAMES, of that Ilk, testament, 1669. C.L. [NRS]

HORSBURGH, ALEXANDER, of that Ilk, sasines, 1750-1751. [NRS.RS18.13.45/48; 11.60/144]

HOUSE, WILLIAM, a mason in Duns, sasine, 1774. [NRS.RS18.16.360]

HOUSTON, LUDOVIC, in Selkirk, a deed, 1757. [NRS.CC18.7.117]

HOWIESON, WILLIAM, feuar in Duns, sasines, 1682-1684. [NRS.RS18.4.321/322/425]

HOWISON, DAVID, in Duns, testament, 1673. [C.L. [NRS]

HOWLATSON, ALEXANDER, in Braehead, Lauder, testament, 1698. C.L. [NRS]

HOWNAM, or USHER, ISABEL, in Darnick, deeds, 1756/1757. [NRS.CC18.7.30/112]

HOWNAM, JOHN, portioner of Darnick, deeds, 1756/1757. [NRS.CC18.7.30/111]

HOWNAME, WALTER, from Teviotdale, a Covenanter transported from Leith to Jamaica in August 1685, landed in Port Royal, Jamaica. [RPCS.II.330][LJ]

HOY, ROBERT, merchant in Coldstream, sasines, 1710/1755. [NRS.RS18.8.120; 13.480]

HOY, ROBERT, in Coldstream, testament, 1664. C.L. [NRS]

The People of the Scottish Borders, 1650-1800

HOY, WILLIAM, portioner in Gattonside, grandson and heir to William Hoy a portioner there, 1792. [NRS.S/H]

HUIE, JAMES, born 1740, an Excise officer in Kelso, died 3 July 1809, husband of Isabella Smith died 3 April 1816. [Kelso MI]

HULDIE, GEORGE, a sailor in Ayton, sasines, 1750-1776. [NRS.RS18.13.28; 15.137; 17.70]

HULDIE, PATRICK, portioner of Ayton, sasines, 1709-1715. [NRS.RS18.7.544/559/561/; 8.594/596]

HUME, ALEXANDER, minister of Abbey St Bathans, 1755-1758, minister at Polwarth, from 1758. [F.2.3]

HUME, DAVID, portioner of Westruther, and his spouse Elizabeth Bell, a deed, 1715. [NRS.RD2.104.560]

HUME, HARRY, commissar clerk of Lauder, deeds, 1715. [NRS.RD3.146.362; RD4.117.190]

HUME, JAMES, in Chapelhill, a deed, 1756. [NRS.CC18.7.46]

HUME, Sir JOHN, of Blackadder, deeds, 1715. [NRS.RD2.105.505; RD4.116.182]

HUME, JOHN, in Highchestermiln, a deed, 1757. [NRS.CC18.7.86]

HUME, Sir PATRICK, of Lumsden, an advocate, deeds, 1715. [NRS.RD3.144.459/500; RD4.116.860]

HUME, WILLIAM, minister at Jedburgh from 1674 to 1681. [F.2.126]

HUME, WILLIAM, in Mebonlaw, a deed, 1757. [NRS.CC18.7.123]

HUME, WILLIAM, born 1715, a heritor in Duns, died 11 August 1797, his spouse Agnes Cairns died 1784. [Duns MI, Berwickshire]

HUNTER, ALEXANDER, feuar and merchant in Duns, testament, 1755. C.L. [NRS]

HUNTER, EDGAR, son of Dr William Hunter in Linthill, sasine, 1779. [NRS.RS18.17.377]

The People of the Scottish Borders, 1650-1800

HUNTER, GEORGE, born 1713, died 22 September 1770. [Abbey St Bathans MI, Berwickshire]

HUNTER, JAMES, a merchant in Duns, testaments, 1750/1764. C.L. [NRS]

HUNTER, JAMES, son of James Hunter in Duns, Berwickshire, emigrated before 1756, settled in King George County, Virginia, sasines, 1776. [NRS.SH.1756; RS19.17.32/39]

HUNTER, JAMES, servant to Alexander Glen minister at Kirkton, a deed, 1758. [NRS.CC18.7.129]

HUNTER, JAMES, a merchant in Duns, 1785. [NRS.E326.4.1]

HUNTER, JOHN, a shoemaker in Berwick, sasines, 1757. [NRS.RS18.13.518/519]

HUNTER, JOHN, born 1733, tenant in Godacroft, died 23 January 1805, his spouse Elizabeth Mack, born 1750, died at Reston on 22 October 1822. [Abbey St Bathans MI, Berwickshire]

HUNTER, ROBERT, a merchant in Eyemouth, testament, 1770. C.L. [NRS]

HUNTER, WILLIAM, of Linthill, born 1657, educated at Edinburgh University, minister at Lilliesleaf from 1695 until his death on 13 November 1736; husband of (1) Alison Hog, parents of Alison, (2) Margaret Potts, parents of William and Margaret. [F.2.183]

HUNTER, WILLIAM, a writer in Melrose, a deed, 1758. [NRS.CC18.7.146]

HUNTER, WILLIAM, of Linthill, MD, sasines, 1779. [NRS.RS18.17.309/375/376/377]

HUNTLIE, THOMAS, grieve at Duns Castle, testament, 1788. C.L. [NRS]

HUNTLY, THOMAS, son and heir of Thomas Huntly a feuar in Denholm and late tenant in Honeyburn, 1796. [NRS.S/H]

HUTCHISON, AGNES, spouse of William Fairbairn a mason in Coldstream, a sasine, 1780. [NRS.RS18.17.409]

HUTCHISON, JOHN, in Paxton, testament, 1771. C.L. [NRS]

The People of the Scottish Borders, 1650-1800

HUTCHISON, Captain RICHARD, in Jedburgh, a deed of factory, 1759. [NRS.CC18.7.206]

HUTTON, JAMES, tenant in Chapel, testament, 1738, C.L. [NRS]

HUTTON, Dr JAMES, of Sleighhouses, a sasine, 1760. [NRS.RS18.14.260]

HUTTON, JOHN, son of James Hutton in Chapel Lauder, Berwickshire, emigrated from Leith aboard the Caledonia to Darien, 14 July 1698, testament, 1707, Edinburgh. [NRS.CC8.8.83]

HYMMER, AGNES, spouse of John Johnston a clothier in Coldstream, a sasine, 1701. [NRS.RS18.6.250]

IDINTON, ANNA, relict of George Lourie in Coldingham, testament, 1673. C.L. [NRS]

IDINTON, GEORGE, feuar in Coldingham, testament, 1745. C.L. [NRS]

INGLIS, ARCHIBALD, minister at Ashkirk, Selkirkshire, from 1675 to 1685. [F.2.169]

INGLIS, JAMES, a weaver in Eyemouth, testament, 1782. C.L. [NRS]

INGLIS, THOMAS, in Selkirk, 1783. [NRS.E326.1.210]

INGLIS, WILLIAM, in Eccles, testament, 1672. C.L. [NRS]

INGLIS, WILLIAM, a weaver in Eyemouth, a sasine, 1780. [NRS.RS18.17.429]

INGRAM, PATRICK, a weaver in Ayton, a sasine, 1766. [NRS.RS18.15.208]

INNERWICK, NICOLAS, in Chirnside, testament, 1686. C.L. [NRS]

INNERWICK, WILLIAM, of Whitsome, a portioner, sasines, 1677-1716. [NRS.RS18.4.10, ETC]

INNES, COLIN, schoolmaster at Duns, testament, 1709. C.L. [NRS]

INNES, JAMES, jailer of Jedburgh prison, 1739. [NRS.CS228.B.2.95]

INNES, WILLIAM, of Sandside, a sasine, 1769. [NRS.RS18.15.410]

The People of the Scottish Borders, 1650-1800

IRVINE, ANDREW, born 1700, tenant in Monkscroft, died 13 May 1756; his spouse Bessie Turnbull, born 1702, died 26 October 1768. [Cavers MI]

IRVIN, THOMAS, born 1677, late tenant in Whitehaugh, died 1739; his spouse Jean Irvin, born 1691, died 11 February 1765. [Cavers MI]

IRVINE, WALTER, born 1740, merchant in Hawick, died 17 March 1806; his spouse Janet Smith, died 2 December 1818. [Cavers MI]

IRVINE, WILLIAM, born 1726, late magistrate of Hawick, died 2 February 1803. [Cavers MI]

JACK, WILLIAM, minister at Kelso, 1695 until his death after October 1699. [F.2.72]

JACKSON, DOROTHEA, heir to her father Dr Charles Jackson of Nicholastown near Kelso, 1787. [NRS.S/H]

JACKSON, JAMES, an Excise Officer at Coldstream, later a merchant there, sasines, 1743-1769. [NRS.RS18.12.30, etc]

JACKSON, JOHN, born 1661, herd in Adderston Shiels, died 27 December 1712, his son James Jackson, born 1705, died in Fultorum, 27 December 1739. [Cavers MI]

JACOBSON, JOHN, in Birgham later in Spittleheugh, and his spouse Janet Dods, sasines, 1764/1764. [NRS.RS18.14/512; 16/362]

JAFFREY, GEORGE, a butcher and feuar in Duns, testament, 1771. C.L. [NRS]

JAFFREY, WILLIAM, in Raburn, testament, 1675. C.L. [NRS]

JAFFREY, WILLIAM, born 1698, a smith in Butterdean, died 7 March 1769, his spouse Annie, born 1731, died 27 November 1788. [Abbey St Bathans MI, Berwickshire]

JAMESON, PATRICK, carrier in Renton, testament, 1749. C.L. [NRS]

JAMESON, WILLIAM, in Mersington, testament, 1671. C.L. [NRS]

JAMIESON, ADAM, a merchant in Whitsome, sasines, 1683/1687. [NRS.RS18.4/357-359; 5/12]

JAMIESON, JAMES, of Herdrig, a surgeon in Kelso, a sasine, 1762. [NRS.RS18.14.395]

JAMIESON, JOHN, minister at Eccles 1654-1662. [F.2.13]

JAMIESON, ROBERT, a skinner in Duns, a sasine, 1679. [NRS.RS18.4.163]

JEFFREY, ANDREW, a shoemaker and tanner in Polwarth, a sasine, 1772. [NRS.RS18.16.206]

JEFFREY, GEORGE, a butcher in Duns, sasines, 1766-1780. [NRS.RS18.15.178/472/429]

JEFFREY, PATRICK, a butcher in Duns, sasines, 1766/1780. [NRS.RS18.15.178; 17.429]

JEFFRIES, WILLIAM, of Sunwick, formerly called Hutton Bell, parish of Hutton, testament, 1780. C.L. [NRS]

JERDAN, ANDREW, gardener at Paston, heir to his father Andrew Jerdan, gardener at Bongate, second son of the deceased Andrew Jerdan, the elder, gardener at Bongate, 1770. [NRS.S/H]

JERDAN, JOHN, bailie of Kelso, heir to his father John Jerdan, a tanner and feuar there, 1790. [NRS.S/H]

JERDAN, RICHARD, gardener in Bongate, heir to his grandfather Richard Jerdan a gardener there, 1798. [NRS.S/H]

JERDONE, ARCHIBALD, of Bonjedward, a deed, 1761. [NRS.CC18.7.308]

JERDONE, ARCHIBALD, factor for Colonel William Elliot of Wells, a deed of factory, 1758. [NRS.CC18.7.180]

JERDONE, FRANCIS, born 30 January 1720, son of John Jerdone a factor and merchant in Jedburgh, emigrated to America in 1746, settled in Hampton, Yorktown, and Louisa County, Virginia, died 5 August 1771. [Louisa MI] [WMQ.2.11.10]

JERDONE, JOHN, a merchant in Jedburgh, a deed, 1757. [NRS.CC18.7.104]

The People of the Scottish Borders, 1650-1800

JOHNSTONE, ALEXANDER, portioner of Coldingham, sasines, 1762/1770. [NRS.RS18.14.383; 15.468]

JOHNSTONE, ALEXANDER, minister at Cranshaws from 1792 to 1801. [F.2.7]

JOHNSTON, Captain ARCHIBALD, a shopkeeper in Kelso, 1785. [NRS.E326.4.1]

JOHNSTONE, GEORGE, minister at Earlston, testaments, 1703-1707. C.L. [NRS]

JOHNSTONE, JAMES, from Spotswood, Berwickshire, emigrated to East New Jersey in 1684, settled at Pitscataway. [Insh.264]

JOHNSTONE, JAMES, tenant in Easterlaws, testament, 1722. C.L. [NRS]

JOHNSTON, JAMES, born 1732, died 13 March 1784, his wife Alison Hately, born 1732, died 7 October 1804, son John, born 1757, died 31 August 1820. [Abbey St Bathans MI, Berwickshire]

JOHNSTONE, JOHN, a skipper in Coldingham, a sasine, 1658. [NRS.RS18.4.34]

JOHNSTONE, JOHN, a clothier in Coldstream, a sasine 1701. [NRS.RS18.6.250]

JOHNSTONE, JOHN, a gardener in Wedderburn, a sasine, 1772. [NRS.RS8.16.211]

JOHNSTONE, JOHN, a riding surveyor in Eyemouth, a sasine, 1770. [NRS.RS18.16.39]

JOHNSTONE, LAURENCE, born 1674, minister at Duns from 1703 until his death in 1736, spouse of (1) Grizel Hunter, (2) Jean Trotter, [F.2.10]; sasines, 1709-1724, [NRS.RS18.7.576; 9.514; 10.48]; testament, 1737. C.L. [NRS]

JOHNSTONE, NICOL, in Chirnside, a sasine, 1759. [NRS.RS18.14.28]

JOHNSTONE, PATRICK, a tailor in Duns, testament, 1678. C.L. [NRS]

JOHNSTONE, PATRICK, born 1653, died 1 May 1698, his wife Jean Moffat born 1647, died 11 April 1723. [Abbey St Bathans MI, Berwickshire]

JOHNSTONE, ROBERT, a baker in Coldstream, sasines, 1765-1776. [NRS.RS18.15.96; 16.130, 201, 396; 17.58, 62]

The People of the Scottish Borders, 1650-1800

JOHNSTONE, THOMAS, a barber and wigmaker in Coldstream, a sasine, 1765. [NRS.RS18.15.93]

JOHNSTONE, WILLIAM, a merchant in Coldstream, testament, 1746. C.L. [NRS]

JOHNSTONE, WILLIAM, a surgeon in Coldstream, sasines, 1758/1778, [NRS.RS18.17.214]; testament, 1778. C.L. [NRS]

JOLLY, JOHN, minister at Coldingham, sasines, 1766-1773. [NRS.RS18.15.217; 16.246]

JORDAN, JOHN, a tanner in Kelso, Roxburghshire, 1768-1774. [NRS.CS96.3835]

JUNIOR, ALEXANDER, a writer in Duns, a sasine, 1774. [NRS.RS18.16.365]

KAE, ALEXANDER, late servant to John Morison Hume of Coldingham Law, testament, 1742. C.L. [NRS]

KARR, JOHN, miller at Foulden Mylne, testament, 1655. C.L. [NRS]

KATCHEAN, JAMES, born 25 December 1797, ordained as minister of the Gospel at Belleville, Canada, 1831, minister of the Free Church in Mordington, Berwickshire, 1844, died 30 November 1871. [Mordington MI]

KAY, DAVID, a tailor in Ayton, a sasine, 1761. [NRS.RS18.14.327]

KAY, WILLIAM, a feuar in Coldingham, a sasine, 1748. [NRS.RS18.12.446]

KEDDIE, MARION, spouse to George Johnstone in Gordon, testament, 1681. C.L. [NRS]

KEIR, ELIZABETH, spouse to Alexander Dickson in Welrig, testament, 1672. C.L. [NRS]

KEIR, JAMES, a shopkeeper in Kelso, 1785. [NRS.E326.4.1]

KEITH, JOHN, a merchant in Eyemouth, testaments, 1771-1772. C.L. [NRS]

KEITH, WALTER, minister at Ginilkirk, testament, 1683. C.L. [NRS]

KELLIE, JOHN, portioner of Coldingham, a sasine, 1668. [NRS.RS18.3.418]

KELLO, WILLIAM, in Ridbraes, testament, 1667. C.L. [NRS]

The People of the Scottish Borders, 1650-1800

KENNEDY, JOHN, in Littlethank, testament, 1670. C.L. [NRS]

KENNEDY, ROBERT, from Tweed-dale, a member of the Scots Charitable Society of Boston 1762. [NEHGS]

KENULTOURS, GEORGE, in Whitsom, testament, 1665. C.L. [NRS]

KERR, AGNES, in Lustruther, a bond, 1761. [NRS.CC18.7.339]

KERR, ANDREW, tenant in South Side of Mersington, testament, 1730. C.L. [NRS]

KERR, ANDREW, in Nether Chatto, a deed, 1757. [NRS.CC18.7.96]

KERR, CHARLES, in Greens Liddisdale, deeds, 1757. [NRS.CC18.7.103/110/119]

KERR, CHARLES, in South Dean Miln, bonds, 1757-1761. [NRS.CC18.7.90/339]

KERR, CHARLES, only son of the deceased Charles Kerr, late tenant in South Dean Mill, heir to his uncle William Kerr, tenant in Luthstruther, 1766. [NRS.S/H]

KERR, CHARLES, of Wells, Roxburghshire, 1770. [NRS.CS228.A.3.48]

KER, GILBERT, the younger of Gateshaw, born 1749, died 26 March 1832, his wife Margaret Hood died 22 August 1785. [Kelso MI]

KERR, HENRY, born 1702, from Graden, Teviotdale, an officer of the Spanish Army from 1722 to 1728, returned to Scotland in 1745 to fight for the Jacobites, captured and banished from Scotland in 1748, died in 1751. [NRS.NRAS#NA6719]

KERR, JAMES, a tailor in Dodsland near Kelso, husband of Margaret Dods died 1694, parents of John, Isabel and Jane, circa 1700. [NRS.SQR.K17]

KERR, JAMES, miller at Foulden Miln, a sasine, 1774. [NRS.RS18.16.322]

KERR, JOHN, a surgeon in Kelso, a sasine, 1731. [NRS.RS18]

KERR, MARK, of Blackburn, sasine, 1710, [NRS.RS18.8.107]; testament, 1710. C.L. [NRS]

The People of the Scottish Borders, 1650-1800

KERR, MARK, an Excise officer in Duns, sasines, 1753-1755. [NRS.RS18.13.324/462]

KERR, MARTHA, relict of James Rutherford a surgeon in Jedburgh, testament, 1763. C.L. [NRS]

KERR, STROTHER, of Littledean, sasines, 1772-1778. [NRS.RS18.16.152; 16.189; 17.260]

KERR, Sir WALTER, of Fadonside, a sasine, 1665. [NRS.RS18.1.257]

KERR, WALTER, a merchant in Duns, testaments, 1735/1736/1741. C.L. [NRS]

KERR, WILLIAM, in Cleughheid, a deed, 1758. [NRS.CC18.7.148]

KERR, WILLIAM, in Lustruther, bonds, 1757. [NRS.CC18.7.90/125]

KER, WILLIAM, of Gateshaw, born 1707, died 25 April 1794, his wife Elizabeth, daughter of Gilbert Elliot of Stonedge, born 1720, died 9 September 1768. [Kelso MI]

KERSE, ISOBEL, spouse to Robert Rankine in Swinton, testament, 1671. C.L. [NRS]

KERSE, MUNGO, in Swinton, testament, 1668. C.L. [NRS]

KERSE, ROBERT, a cooper in Coldstream, a sasine, 1762. [NRS.RS18.14.428]

KERSE, WILLIAM, a fish-cooper in Coldstream, a sasine, 1761. [NRS.RS18.14.374]

KILPATRICK, SAMUEL, minister at Ladykirk, testament, 1714. C.L. [NRS]

KING, ANDREW, in Coldingham, a sasine, 1665. [NRS.RS18.1.279]

KING, HERCULES, in Bogengrein, a sasine, 1655. [NRS.RS18.4.22]

KING, JOHN, in Little Swinton, testament, 1653. C.L. [NRS]

KING, JOHN, born 1736, factor on Ayton Estate, died 20 November 1816. [Ayton MI, Berwickshire]

KINGHORN, DAVID, in Coldstream, testament, 1663. C.L. [NRS]

The People of the Scottish Borders, 1650-1800

KINGHORN, DAVID, a maltman in Coldstream, a sasine, 1753. [NRS.RS18.13.318]

KINGHORN, GEORGE, a dragoon of the Scots Greys, a sasine, 1753. [NRS.RS18.13.318]

KINGHORN, JAMES, feuar in Coldstream, testament, 1748. C.L. [NRS]

KINNEAR, ALEXANDER, born around 1627, minister at Hawick 1663-1667, husband of Margaret Cunningham. [F.2.113]

KIRKINGTON, JOHN, in Coldstream, his spouse Isobel Nisbet, and their son John Kirkington, a sasine, 1668. [NRS.RS18.2.118]

KIRKPATRICK, THOMAS, and his spouse Marion Cockburn, in Coldstream, 1710. [NRS.RS18.8.120]

KIRKTON, JOHN, born 1628, from Mertoun, Berwickshire, a minister in exile in Rotterdam from 1676-1687. [SEC]

KIRKWOOD, GEORGE, town clerk of Lauder, testament, 1740. C.L. [NRS]

KIRKWOOD, JOHN, a watchmaker in Ridpath, and his spouse Mary Tait, a sasine, 1759. [NRS.RS18.14.132]

KNOWLES, PATRICK, son of Christopher Knowles of Swynwood, sasines, 1669-1712. [NRS.RS18.2.176; 3.335; 8.328]

KNOX, ALEXANDER, in Paxton, a sasine, 1660. [NRS.RS18.4.135]

KNOX, JANET, born 1738, spouse to Alexander Mackay, died 9 February 1804. [Ayton MI, Berwickshire]

KNOX, JOHN, a skinner in Duns, a sasine, 1773. [NRS.RS18.16.283]

KNOX, JOHN, born 1731, a weaver and feuar in Duns, died 9 June 1804, his spouse Susan Forsyth, born 1740, died 20 May 1782. [Duns MI, Berwickshire]

KNOX, ROBERT, in Easter Woodheads of Waderly, testament, 1706. C.L. [NRS]

KNOX, WILLIAM, a merchant in Eyemouth, a sasine, 1767. [NRS.RS18.15.242]

KYLE, DAVID, portioner of Lessudden, a deed, 1760. [NRS.CC18.7.296]

The People of the Scottish Borders, 1650-1800

KYLE, JOHN, in Earlston, testament, 1690. C.L. [NRS]

KYLE, ROBERT, born 1757, resident of Kelso, died 1782, his spouse Mary Anderson, born 1747, died 18 December 1822. [Kelso MI]

KYLE, THOMAS, born 1681, portioner of Earlston, died 1724. [Earlston MI]

LACKIE, ANDREW, a shopkeeper in Kelso, 1785. [NRS.E326.4.1]

LAIDLAW, JAMES, carrier in Hawick, a deed, 1758. [NRS.CC18.7.172]

LAIDLAW, JOHN, in Unthank, a deed, 1759. [NRS.CC18.7.223]

LAIDLAW, JOHN, born 1794 in Roxburghshire, a teacher, with his wife Agnes a teacher from Edinburgh, settled in Brooklyn, New York, naturalised 24 July 1820.

LAIDLAW, THOMAS, in Barns, testament, 1723. C.L. [NRS]

LAIDLIE, ARCHIBALD, born in Kelso, Roxburghshire, educated at Edinburgh University 1730, a Dutch Reformed minister in New York 1734-1776, died at Red Hook, New York, 1779. [CCMC]

LAIDLIE, MARGARET, in Thirlstane, testament, 1685. C.L. [NRS]

LAING, WILLIAM, from Hawick, Roxburghshire, a Covenanter transported from Leith to New York 19 May 1684. [RPCS.8.216]

LAING, WILLIAM, minister at Ligertwood, a sasine, Stichill, 1703. [NRS.RS18.6.438]

LAMB, AGNES and MARGARET, only children of John Lamb, cooper in Denholm, and his wife Ann Johnston, heirs to their grandfather John Johnston a workman in Denholm, 1771. [NRS.S/H]

LAMB, ELIZABETH, wife of Andrew Busby a wright in Kelso, died 1688. [NRS.Scottish Quaker Records, K17.119]

LAMB, EUPHAN, in Quainscairn, Stitchil, a Quaker, 1684. [RPCS.3.IX.681]

LAMB, GEORGE, of Old Greenlaw, sasines, 1715-1733, [NRS.RS18.9.48/50; 10.273; 11.32/34]; testament, 1736. C.L. [NRS]

The People of the Scottish Borders, 1650-1800

LAMB, JAMES, in Stichill, 1684, died 1701, his wife Margaret Busby died 1704, parents of Samuel born 1688. [NRS.SQR.K17]

LAMB, JAMES, from Teviotdale, a member of the Scots Charitable Society of Boston 1750. [NEGHS]

LAMB, JANET, a Quaker in Maxwellheugh, died 1675. [NRS.SQR.K17]

LAMB, ..., his wife Christian Grieve died in Stitchill 1683, parents of James. [NRS.Scottish Quaker Records, k17.118]

LANDELL, GEORGE RICHARDSON, born 1785, a Lieutenant of the Royal Marines, died in Montreal on 8 August 1834, son of Rev. James Landell, minister at Coldingham, Berwickshire, and his wife Janet Heriot. [Coldingham MI]

LANDELL, JAMES, born 1783, a Lieutenant of the 60th Regiment, died at Port Antonio, Jamaica, 26 July 1803, son of Rev. James Landell minister at Coldingham, Berwickshire, and his wife Janet Heriot. [Coldingham MI]

LANDELL, THOMAS, born 1786, died in Jamaica, 25 November 1815, son of Rev. James Landell minister at Coldingham, Berwickshire, and his wife Janet Heriot. [Coldingham MI]

LANDELLS, DAVID, a weaver in Coldingham, a sasine, 1667. [NRS.RS18.2.38]

LANDELLS, JOHN, tenant of Gunsgreen, testament, 1799. C.L. [NRS]

LANDRETH, GEORGE, in Gladswood, a deed, 1758. [NRS.CC18.7.146]

LANDRETH, JAMES, minister at Simprin, testament, 1756. C.L. [NRS]

LANDRETH, PATRICK, son of John Landreth in Coldstream, a sasine, 1671. [NRS.RS18.2.340]

LANDRETH, THOMAS, in Corsflat, deeds, 1758-1759. [NRS.CC18.7.146/206/213]

LANG, JANET, spouse to John Adamson the elder in Duns, testament, 1680. C.L. [NRS]

LANG, Mrs, in Selkirk, 1783. [NRS.E326.1.210]

The People of the Scottish Borders, 1650-1800

LANGLANDS, JOHN, born 1633, minister at Hawick 1667-1689, died 24 May 1707, husband of Margaret Rutherford, parents of Robert, John, Margaret, Alison, and Margaret. [F.2.114]

LANGLANDS, JOHN, M.D., heir to his father John Langlands, minister at Hawick, 1707. [NRS.S/H]

LANGLANDS, WALTER, chamberlain to Sir Walter Scott of Harden, parish of Merton, testament, 1698. C.L. [NRS]

LANSON, JOHN, in Mosspaldgreen, deeds, 1758-1761. [NRS.CC18.7.149/337]

LAUDER, Sir ARCHIBALD, of Edington, testament, 1705. C.L. [NRS]

LAUDER, CHARLES, town clerk of Lauder, sasine, 1702, [NRS.RS18.6.378]; testament, 1705. C.L. [NRS]

LAUDER, Sir JOHN, of Edington, sasines, 1697-1698. [NRS.RS18.5.337/374]

LAUDER, JOHN, minister at Eccles 1691, died 1729, spouse of Margaret Borthwick, [F.2.14]; testaments, 1731, 1735, 1739. C.L. [NRS]

LAUDER, PATRICK, in Coldstream, a sasine, 1708. [NRS.RS18.7.372]

LAUDER, WILLIAM, treasurer of Lauder, a sasine, 1763. [NRS.RS18.14.437]

LAURIE, DAVID, clerk to James Grieve postmaster at Berwick, a sasine, 1764. [NRS.RS18.14.504]

LAURIE, JAMES, a maltman in Duns, a sasine, 1663. [NRS.RS18.1.99]

LAUTIE, JAMES, minister at Chirnside, testament, 1695. C.L. [NRS]

LAURIE, JAMES, born 1704, minister at Hawick from 1757 until his death on 23 December 1783, husband of Elizabeth Foggo, parents of John, Mary, and Elizabeth. [F.2.115]

LAW, DAVID, from Innerleithen, Peebles-shire, a member of the Scots Charitable Society of Boston 1734. [NEGHS]

LAW, PATRICK, in Duns, a sasine, 1663. [NRS.RS18.1.66]

LAW, WILLIAM, of Elvington, sasines, 1733-1743. [NRS.RS18.11.110; 12.41]

The People of the Scottish Borders, 1650-1800

LAWSON, ALEXANDER, wright in Hilton, testament, 1671. C.L. [NRS]

LAWSON, JOHN, miller at Oldcambus Mylne, sasines, 1713-1724. [NRS.RS18.8.444; 10.45]

LEARMONTH, JANET, relict of John Chartres, in Coldstream, testament, 1750. C.L. [NRS]

LEARMONT, AGNES, and SARAH, daughters of the deceased James Learmont in Kelso, heirs to their grandfather George Learmont a weaver in Kelso, 1789. [NRS.S/H]

LEARMONTH, JOHN, of that Ilk, testament, 1680. C.L. [NRS]

LEARMONTH, PATRICK, in Wedderlie, testament, 1652. C.L. [NRS]

LEARMONTH, PATRICK, a weaver in Duns, sasines, 1683-1715. [NRS.RS18.4.381; 9.31]

LEARMONTH, THOMAS, in Greenlaw, a sasine, 1760. [NRS.RS18.14.272]

LEE, AGNES, relict of Alexander Marshall in Home, testament, 1734. C.L. [NRS]

LEGGAT, GIDEON, in Easter Swanshiel, deeds, 1758. [NRS.CC18.7.128/129]

LEGGAT, GIDEON, in Unthank, a deed, 1759. [NRS.CC18.7.204]

LEGGAT, WALTER, born 1785 in Hawick, Roxburghshire, a merchant in New York 1827, died there on 30 September 1850. [StAndrews Soc.NY.I.24]

LEITCH, JAMES, a merchant in Home, testaments, 1729, 1730, 1736. C.L. [NRS]

LEITCH, JOHN, and his spouse Margaret Purves, in Home, a sasine, 1760. [NRS.RS18.14.272]

LEITCH, JOHN, born 1758, died 3 January 1796, husband of Ann Jamieson, born 1748, died 25 April 1824. [Kelso MI]

LEITCH, PATRICK, and his spouse Margaret Hogg, in Ladykirk, testament, 1693. C.L. [NRS]

LEITHHEAD, WILLIAM, in Whitlaw, Hawick, heir to his uncle Walter Leithhead, a smith in Jamaica, 1764. [SHR.28]

The People of the Scottish Borders, 1650-1800

LEITHOLM, JOHN, in Ayton, sasines, 1767-1768. [NRS.RS18.15.247/292]

LERMENT, JOHN, born 1729, miller in Hume Miln, died 19 January 1803, husband of Helen Anderson, born 1729, died 10 March 1802. [Earlston MI]

LERMONT, JOHN, born 1707, died 12 September 1780. [Earlston MI]

LIDDELL, DAVID, son of James Liddell, a glover in Duns, a sasine, 1728. [NRS.RS18.10.290]

LIDDELL, JOHN, a glover in Duns, testament, 1667. C.L. [NRS]

LIDDELL, JOHN, a merchant in Duns, testament, 1701. C.L. [NRS]

LIDDELL, MARGARET, daughter of James Liddell in Duns, and spouse of Robert Balfour a notary there, a sasine, 1663. [NRS.RS18.1.64]

LIDDERDAINE, ISOBEL, spouse to William Stirling in Earlston, testament, 1653. C.L. [NRS]

LIDDERDALE, JOHN, treasurer of the burgh of Selkirk, a sasine, 1650. [NRS.RS18.3.453]

LIDDESS, ADAM, in Cruikfoord, testament, 1653. C.L. [NRS]

LIE, JOHN, tenant in Snook Milne, testament, 1718. C.L. [NRS]

LIGHTHARNES, JOHN, portioner of Coldingham Law, testament, 1653. C.L. [NRS]

LIGHTHARNES, JOHN, a feuar in Eyemouth, sasines, 1750-1761. [NRS.RS18.13.89/501; 14.362]

LILLIE, Mrs MARGARET, born 1635, wife of William Lillie, died 4 October 1705. [Mindrum MI]

LILLIE, THOMAS, a smith in Sprouston, a sasine, 1717. [NRS.RS18.9.174]

LILLIE, ..., a feuar in Kelso, Roxburghshire, 26 December 1728. [NRS.CS175.380]

LIN, JOHN, in Duns, a sasine, 1664. [NRS.RS18.1.233]

The People of the Scottish Borders, 1650-1800

LINDORES, MARGARET, spouse to James Forsyth in Blackburn, testament, 1684. C.L. [NRS]

LINDSAY, ELIZABETH, from Jedburgh, Roxburghshire, a gypsy transported from Glasgow to Virginia in 1 January 1715. [GR.530]

LINDSAY, THOMAS, in Earlston, testament, 1677. C.L. [NRS]

LITHGOW, JOHN, commissary clerk-depute of Peebles, a sasine, 1687. [NRS.RS18.5.25]

LITHGOW, JOHN, a mason in Greenlaw, a sasine, 1779. [NRS.RS18.17.321]

LITHGOW, ROBERT, born 1680, son of Alexander Lithgow of Drygrange and his wife Margaret Elliot, educated at Edinburgh University 1701, minister at Ashkirk, Selkirkshire, from 1711 until his death on 15 November 1729; husband of Isabella Langlands, parents of Robert. [F.2.169]

LITHGOW, WILLIAM, wright in Newbigging, testament, 1709. C.L. [NRS]

LITSTER, JEAN, in Putten Milne, testament, 1738. C.L. [NRS]

LITSTER, THOMAS, town clerk of Duns, sasine, 1734, [NRS.RS18.11.175]; testament, 1742. C.L. [NRS]

LITTLE, JOHN, a merchant in Langholm, bonds, 1760. [NRS.CC18.7.261/264]

LITTLE, MARION, daughter of Alexander Little in Trabroun, testament, 1741. C.L. [NRS]

LIVINGSTONE, ALEXANDER, in Eyemouth, a sasine, 1669. [NRS.RS18.2.203]

LIVINGSTON, ROBERT, born in Ancrum, Roxburghshire, on 13 December 1654, son of Reverend John Livingston and his wife Janet Fleming, to America 1673, settled in Charlestown, Massachusetts, and later in Albany, New York, a merchant and civil servant, died 1 October 1728.

LOCH, JOHN, in Duns, a sasine, 1672. [NRS.RS18.3.30]

LOCH, MARK, in Swinton, testament, 1679. C.L. [NRS]

LOCKIE, JOHN, in Martine, a sasine, 1675. [NRS.RS18.3.273]

The People of the Scottish Borders, 1650-1800

LOCKIE, JOHN, a baker in Kelso, Roxburghshire, 1784. [NRS.CS228.A.5.27.1]

LOCKIE, THOMAS, carrier in Jedburgh, a bond, 1758. [NRS.CC18.7.153]

LOCKY, THOMAS, born 1686, tenant in Dalcove, died 1741, his spouse Agnes Henderson, born 1684, died January 1741. [Mertoun MI, Berwickshire]

LOGAN, GEORGE, of Burncastle, sasines, 1670-1715. [NRS.RS18.2.220, etc]

LOGAN, JAMES, a glover in Duns, sasines, 1696-1705. [NRS.RS18.5.308; 7.100]

LOGAN, JOHN, of Burncastle, a sasine, 1670, [NRS.RS18.2.220]; testament, 1672. C.L. [NRS]

LOOKUP, ANDREW, burgess and bailie of Jedburgh, heir to his brother George Lookup, a surgeon in London, lately residing at the Hague, Holland, 1771. [NRS.S/H]

LOOKUP, GEORGE, a wright in Jedburgh, a deed, 1758. [NRS.CC18.7.177]

LORAINE, ALEXANDER, a feuar and notary in Duns, testaments, 1699/1709. C.L. [NRS]

LORAIN, JAMES, of Angelraw, Sheriff Clerk of Berwickshire, born July 1716, died March 1785. [Duns MI, Berwickshire]; sasines, 1766-1776. [NRS.RS18.15.222/224/228; 16.30/283/284/414; 17.4; etc]

LORRAIN, JOHN, a wigmaker in Duns, a sasine, 1759. [NRS.RS18.14.71]

LORAIN, ROBERT, born 1745, died 15 August 1822, husband of Mary Aitchison, born 1747, died 18 March 1826. [Coldingham MI, Berwickshire]

LORRAINE, WILLIAM, a candle-maker in Duns, sasines, 1745-1759. [NRS.RS12.141; 14.71]

LORIMER, JAMES, minister at Kelso, 1683-1686. [F.2.71]

LORIMER, or WALLACE, JAMES, feuar in Coldingham, a sasine, 1755. [NRS.RS18.13.347]

The People of the Scottish Borders, 1650-1800

LORIMER, JAMES, minister at Yarrow from 1765 until his death on 21 November 1775; husband of (1) Elizabeth Oswald, parents of Janet, Helen, Elizabeth, and Oswald, (2) Jean Sibbald, parents of James. [F.2.197]

LOTHIAN, ALEXANDER, a burgess of Lauder, a sasine, 1762. [NRS.RS18.14.424]

LOTHIAN, WILLIAM, bailie of Trabroun and factor for the Earl of Lauderdale, testaments, 1726/1727/1728/1729/1735/1738/1744/1747. C.L. [NRS]

LOWIS, THOMAS, minister at Galashiels 1654-1662, and from 1690-1691, at Innerleithen 1697- . [F.2.177]

LUDGATE, ROBERT, shoemaker in Coldingham, testament, 1795. C.L. [NRS]

LUDGATE, WILLIAM, a gardener in Coldstream, a sasine, 1769. [NRS.RS18.15.381]

LUMSDALE, JOHN, in Lauder, testament, 1760. C.L. [NRS]

LUMSDEN, ANDREW, millwright at Newstead, son and heir to James Lumsden, miller at Newstead Mill, 1777. [NRS.S/H]

LUMSDEN, PATRICK, a tailor in Coldingham, a sasine, 1667. [NRS.RS18.1.369]

LUNAM, ROBERT, a baker in Greenlaw, sasines, 1752-1756. [NRS.RS18.13.199/485/488/515]

LUNAM, WILLIAM, born 1773, a mason, son of David Lunam, died 17 April 1790. [Duns MI, Berwickshire]

LUNDIE, AGNES, relict of Thomas Heastie a messenger in Duns, testament, 1743. C.L. [NRS]

LUNDIE, ALEXANDER, son of James Lundie of Huttonspittell, sasines, 1669. [NRS.RS18.2.121/122]

LUNDIE, CORNELIUS, born 11 August 1716, son of Archibald Lundie minister at Saltoun, minister at Kelso from 1750 until his death on 17 January 1800, husband of Mary Ronald, parents of Mary, Archibald, Jean, Margaret, Rachel, William, Robert, Elizabeth, Marion, and Catherine. [F.2.72]

The People of the Scottish Borders, 1650-1800

LUNDIE, JAMES, son of Allan Lundie, a surgeon apothecary in Duns, a sasine, 1724. [NRS.RS18.10.10]

LUNDIE, JAMES, of Spittle, testament, 1739. C.L. [NRS]

LUNDIE, WILLIAM, of Simprine, sasines, 1671-1680. [NRS.RS18.2.361, etc]

LUNHAM, ROBERT, tenant in Greenlaw Dean, testament, 1736. C.L. [NRS]

LYALL, JOHN, in Cockburnspath, testament, 1678. C.L. [NRS]

LYALL, ROBERT, in Greenmains, Auchencraw, testament, 1791. C.L. [NRS]

LYDEN, JOHN, portioner of Denholm, died 11 February 1776. [Cavers MI]

LYDEN, WILLIAM, born 1733, portioner of Denholm, died 2 May 1798, his spouse Janet Scott, born 1732, died 31 March 1816. [Cavers MI]

LYLE, JOHN, portioner of Hornden, sasines, 1664-1672. [NRS.RS18.1.199, etc]

LYLE, THOMAS, servant to Sir John Sinclair of Longformacus, a sasine, 1733. [NRS.RS18.11.36]

LYLE, WILLIAM, a fisherman in Lumbsden, a sasine, 1707. [NRS.RS18.7.275]

LYNG, WILLIAM, schoolmaster in Duns, testament, 1682. C.L. [NRS]

MCCALL, ANDREW, a tobacconist in Duns, sasines, 1758-1760. [NRS.RS18.13.541; 14.175]

MCCALL, WILLIAM, a mason in Duns, a sasine, 1772. [NRS.RS18.16.166]

MACATNEY, MARGARET, spouse of John Bowmaker, testament, 1676. C.L. [NRS]

MCCLELLAN, PATRICK, son of Patrick McClellan in Coldingham, a sasine, 1755. [NRS.RS18.13.437]

MCCRACKEN, JAMES, a gardener in Coldstream, sasines, 1746-1765. [NRS.RS18.12.224/460; 14.391; 15.90]

MCCRACKEN, JOHN, His Majesty's boatman at Eyemouth, a sasine, 1769. [NRS.RS18.15.371]

The People of the Scottish Borders, 1650-1800

MCCULLOCH, JOHN, a merchant in Denholm, deeds, 1757-1760. [NRS.CC18.7.93/266]

MCDONALD, HUGH, portioner of Paxton, and his spouse Katherine Knox, sasines, 1675-1683. [NRS.RS18.3.348; 4.352]

MCDOUGALL, ALEXANDER, in Birgham, sasines, 1765-1775. [NRS.RS18.15.88; 16.374]

MCDOUGAL, ANDREW, a weaver in Jedburgh, a deed, 1758. [NRS.CC18.7.148]

MCDOUGALL, GEORGE, in Darnchester, a sasine, 1767. [NRS.RS18.15.270]

MCDOUGALL, ROBERT, born 1729, died 1792, husband of Agnes Wallace, born 1719, died 17 February 1798. [Coldingham MI, Berwickshire]; a sasine, 1776. [NRS.RS18.16.453]

MCDOUGALL, ..., born 1718, a glover in Kelso, died 19 April 1792, husband of Elizabeth Taylor, born 1741, died 20 April 1816. [Kelso MI]

MCDOUGAL, THOMAS, born 1732, minister at Makerstoun, 1760 until his death on 20 June 1784, husband of Anne Inglis, parents of David, Ann, Edward, John, Margaret, William, Catherine and Inglis. [F.2.79]

MCDOUGALL, WILLIAM, wright in Kelso, last in Nenthorn, testaments, 1714-1732. C.L. [NRS]

MCDOUGAL, WILLIAM, born 8 May 1777, son of Rev. Thomas McDougal in Makerstoun, died in Antigua on 11 February 1825. [F.2,79]

MCGALL, JAMES, died 12 March 1724. [Coldingham MI, Berwickshire]

MCGALL, JOHN, born 1720, tenant in Hutton Hall Barns, died 24 May 1781. [Coldingham MI, Berwickshire]

MCGALL, JOHN, born 1769, tenant in Chirnside, died 7 January 1823. [Coldingham MI, Berwickshire]

MCGALL, ROBERT, a feuar in Coldingham, a sasine, 1767. [NRS.RS18.15.244]

MCGHIE, JAMES, a gardener in Etal, sasines, 1732-1747. [NRS.RS18.11.3; 12.367]

The People of the Scottish Borders, 1650-1800

MCGHIE, WILLIAM, educated at Edinburgh University, 1693, minister at Selkirk, 1700 until his death on 30 April 1725; husband of Rachel Dunbar, oarents of William, Margaret, and Elizabeth. [F.2.195]

MCINTOSH, ROBERT, a merchant in Eyemouth, testament, 1798. C.L. [NRS]

MACKAY, DANIEL, minister at Jedburgh from 1707 until his death 10 September 1731, husband of ....Cranstoun. [F.2.127]

MCKEEN, GEORGE, in Coldingham, a sasine, 1675. [NRS.RS18.3.250]

MCKIE, ROBERT, in Billie, a sasine, 1665. [NRS.RS18.1.295]

MACKINIER, WILLIAM, carrier in Coldingham, testament, 1714. C.L. [NRS]

MACKNIGHT, JAMES, minister at Jedburgh, 1769-1772. [F.2.127]

MACKNOCHE, JOHN, in Blackadder, a sasine 1664. [NRS.RS18.1.236]

MACLAGAN, FREDERICK, born 31 May 1738, son of Rev. Alexander MacLagan in Dunkeld, minister at Melrose from 1768 until 1788, died 12 August 1818; husband of Christian Turnbull, parents of Alexander, John Blackwood, Hector, Janet, Jean, George, Frederick, William, George, Mary, William, and Christian. [F.2.189]

MCLAGAN, HECTOR, born 26 June 1768 in Melrose, son of Reverend Frederick McLagan and his wife Christian Turnbull, died in Jamaica 11 September 1808. [F.2.188]

MCLEAN, ANDREW, in Langton, a deed, 1758. [NRS.CC18.7.144]

MCLEAN, JAMES, servant to John Hardie minister at Gordon, testament, 1701. C.L. [NRS]

MCLELLAN, ALISON, spouse to William Jameson in East Morrison, testament, 1664. C.L. [NRS]

MCMAFF, JEAN, in Horndean, spouse of George Gibson, testament, 1672. C.L. [NRS]

MCMIN, JOHN, in Earlston, testament, 1697. C.L. [NRS]

The People of the Scottish Borders, 1650-1800

MCNAUCHE, ANDREW, in Blackadder, testament, 1664. C.L. [NRS]

MCNAUGH, JOHN, in Hornden, testament, 1678. C.L. [NRS]

MCQUEEN, LAUCHLAN, Excise officer at Hutton, testament, 1743. C.L. [NRS]

MCQUEEN, SWEEN, a sergeant of the Royal Scots [North British] Dragoons, afterwards in Duns, a sasine, 1745. [NRS.RS18.12.166]

MABON, GEORGE, a cutler in Duns, sasines, 1755. [NRS.RS18.13.415/474]

MABON, JAMES, a weaver in Eyemouth, a sasine, 1705. [NRS.RS18.7.44]

MACK, ADAM, a weaver in Denholm, a deed, 1760. [NRS.CC18.7.297]

MACK, ANDREW, of Whitchester, formerly in Gordon Mains, sasines, 1748-1766. [NRS.RS18.12.426; 13.198/269/510; 14.42/434; 15.203/234]

MACK, ARCHIBALD, a shoemaker in Duns, a sasine, 1750. [NRS.RS18.13.23]

MACK, JOHN, a tenant in Bellyshiel, testament, 1767. C.L. [NRS]

MADDER, JAMES, and his spouse Isabel Loch, in Duns, a sasine, 1694. [NRS.RS18.5.255]

MADDER, WILLIAM, a mason in Jedburgh, a deed, 1756. [NRS.CC18.7.13]

MAIBON, AGNES, wife of James Jack in Kelso, heir to her father James Maiben in Kelso, 1788. [NRS.S/H]

MAIR, ALEXANDER, a tidewaiter in Eyemouth, and his wife Rachael Kellie, a sasine, 1771. [NRS.RS18.16.74]

MAIR, RICHARD, in Halrule, a deed, 1759. [NRS.CC18.7.205]

MAISLET, JOHN, in Lowick, a sasine, 1666. [NRS.RS18.1.346]

MAITLAND, ALEXANDER, in Lauderdale, a deed, 1767. [NRS.RD2.207/2.401]

MAITLAND, CHARLES, of Haltoun, a sasine, 1660. [NRS.RS18.4.137]

MAITLAND, JOHN, bailie of Lauder, a sasine, 1659, [NRS.RS18.4.63]; testament, 1669. C.L. [NRS]

The People of the Scottish Borders, 1650-1800

MALCOLM, WILLIAM, in Nether Howdoun, testament, 1663. C.L. [NRS]

MALTMAN, MARGARET, in Coldingham, testament, 1671. C.L. [NRS]

MALTMAN, ROBERT, in Coldingham, sasine, 1718. [NRS.RS18.9.272]

MANDERSTON, AGNES, eldest sister of John Manderston portioner of Grueldykes, testament, 1699. C.L. [NRS]

MANDERSTON, WILLIAM, feuar in Duns, a sasine, 1666. [NRS.RS18.1.367]

MANUEL, JAMES, in Lamberton Shiels, testament, 1665. C.L. [NRS]

MANUEL, THOMAS, a blacksmith in Duns, a sasine, 1664. [NRS.RS18.1.210]

MANSFIELD, JOHN, servant to Sir John Home of Blackadder, and his wife Janet Learmonth, a sasine, 1674. [NRS.RS18.3.193]

MARJORIBANKS, AGNES, spouse to Hew Allan in Bruntiburn, testament, 1678. C.L. [NRS]

MARJORIBANKS, JAMES, in Duns, formerly in Langbank, sasines, 1697-1699. [NRS.RS18.5.373/424]

MARJORIBANKS, JOHN, a tailor in Newton of Coldstream, a sasine, 1757. [NRS.RS18.13.516]

MARJORIBANKS, JOHN, of Crumrig, testaments, 1760/1778. C.L. [NRS]

MARJORIBANKS, SIMON, of Stainrig, sasines, 1697-1701. [NRS.RS18.5.339; 6.264/266]

MARK, ROBERT, servant to John Elliot of Borthickbrae, a deed, 1759. [NRS.CC18.7.227]

MARK, THOMAS, shoemaker in Duns, and his son William Thomas, sasines, 1734. [NRS.RS18.11.138/140]

MARR, ANDREW, portioner of Redpath, husband of Isabel Lothian, sasines, 1745-1751, [NRS.RS18.12.156, etc]; testament, 1744. C.L. [NRS]

MARR, THOMAS, portioner of Gattinsyde, a sasine, 1700. [NRS.RS18.6.116]

The People of the Scottish Borders, 1650-1800

MARR, WILLIAM, in Fogo, testament, 1664. C.L. [NRS]

MARSHALL, ANDREW, in Fallside Hill, testament, 1782. C.L. [NRS]

MARSHALL, GEORGE, in Duns, a sasine, 1665. [NRS.RS18.1.267]

MARSHALL, JOHN, tenant in Leitholm, testament, 1721. C.L. [NRS]

MARSHALL, ROBERT, gardener in Gloster Hill, sasine, 1704. [NRS.RS18.6.573]

MARSHALL, THOMAS, tenant in Birgham, testament, 1736. C.L. [NRS]

MARTILL, JANET, spouse of George Chisholm in Boune, testament, 1679. C.L. [NRS]

MARTIN, ALEXANDER, of Ravelaw, sasines, 1685-1720. [NRS.RS18.4.468, etc]

MARTIN, EDWARD, in Duns, testament, 1700. C.L.[NRS]

MARTIN, ISABELL, daughter and heir of James Martin a weaver in Gattonside, 1795. [NRS.S/H]

MARTIN, JAMES, born 1740, died 1798. [Ayton MI, Berwickshire]

MARTIN, JAMES, a merchant in Eyemouth, sasines, 1766-1777. [NRS.RS18.15.198; 17.183]

MARTIN, WILLIAM, a tailor in Earlston, testament, 1728. C.L. [NRS]

MARTIN, WILLIAM, a dyster in Netherbyre Waukmill, a sasine, 1753. [NRS.RS18.13.312]

MARTIN, WILLIAM, portioner of Gattonside, a deed, 1761. [NRS.CC18.7.352]

MARTIN, WILLIAM, born 1723, died 28 June 1794, his spouse Isobel Jeffrey, born 1729, died 28 February 1790. [Ayton MI, Berwickshire]

MARTLE, WILLIAM, in Duns, his widow Janet Henderson, and sons John and William, sasine, 1708. [NRS.RS18.7.405]

MASON, ALEXANDER, portioner and maltster in Ayton, testament, 1744. C.L. [NRS]

The People of the Scottish Borders, 1650-1800

MASON, GEORGE, of Clerklies, formerly in Newton Milne, sasines, 1703-1760. [NRS.RS18.6.482, etc]

MASON, JAMES, minister at Yarrow from 1753 until his death on 12 January 1764; husband of Elizabeth Kirkwood, parents of George, Jean, Isabel, and James. [F.2.197]

MASON, JANET, wife of Hendry Hamilton in Stitchill, a Quaker, 1684. [RPCS.3/IX.680]

MASON, JOHN, a maltster in Redpath, testament, 1737. C.L. [NRS]

MASON, ROBERT, a wright in Redpath, sasines, 1753-1780. [NRS.RS18.13.273/485; 17.25/403]

MATHER, JOHN, in Knowsouth, deeds, 1757-1758. [NRS.CC18.7.108/144]

MATHEWSON, JAMES, born 1724, a merchant in Millfield, died 23 June 1809, his spouse Eleanor, born 1740, died 24 March 1817. [Mindrum MI]

MATHEWSON, JOHN, born 1704, tenant in Moneylaws, died 14 December 1764, his wife Grace, born 1709, died 10 March 1772, their sons John, born 1740, died 10 May 1803, and George, born 1737, died 4 March 1804, with his wife Mary, born 1749, died 1 August 1784. [Mindrum MI]

MATHISON, JAMES, a smith in West Nisbet, testament, 1748. C.L. [NRS]

MATHISON, WILLIAM, a cooper in Melrose, and his spouse Janet Friar, a sasine, 1751. [NRS.RS18.13.109]

MAUCHLIN, JEAN, spouse of John Fair a feuar in Coldstream, testament, 1777. C.L. [NRS]

MAUCHLINE, THOMAS, a merchant in Coldingham, and his daughter Janet Mauchline, a sasine, 1669. [NRS.RS18.2.205]

MAUL, ALEXANDER, in Horndean, sasines, 1776-1779. [NRS.RS18.17.55/277]

MAUL, JOHN, of Leetbrae, alias Marlefield, formerly in Hilton, and his spouse Sarah Hogg, sasines, 1773-1780. [NRS.RS18.16.257; 17.312/313/427]

MAW, ANDREW, in Duns, a sasine, 1702. [NRS.RS18.6.302]

The People of the Scottish Borders, 1650-1800

MAW, DAVID, in Greenlaw, a sasine, 1682. [NRS.RS18.4.315]

MAW, GEORGE, a maltman in Duns, a sasine, 1667. [NRS.RS18.2.11]

MAW, JOHN, a smith in Horndean, testament, 1672. C.L. [NRS]

MAXWELL, JOHN, Lieutenant Colonel of the 20th Regiment of Foot, Lennel House, testament, 1772. C.L. [NRS]

MAXWELL, WILLIAM, in Duns, testament, 1659. C.L. [NRS]

MEARNS, MARGARET, spouse of William Robison in Eymouth, testament, 1653. C.L. [NRS]

MEBEN, MARGARET, spouse of Robert Gootra in Bromdykes, testament, 1673. C.L. [NRS]

MEIK, BESSIE, spouse of John Bairnsfather in Nisbet Hill, testament, 1664. C.L. [NRS]

MEIKLE, HELEN, spouse of Thomas Carraby in Boun, testament, 1683. C.L. [NRS]

MEIN, GILBERT, a carrier in Kelso, heir to his father John Mein a carrier there, 1789. [NRS.S/H]

MEINE, HENRY, a merchant in Kelso, Roxburghshire, 1706. [NRS.CS228.A.1.30]

MEIN, JAMES, son of George Mein, a feuar in Coldstream, 1754. [NRS.RS18.13.378]

MEIN, WILLIAM, a feuar in Coldstream, a sasine, 1754. [NRS.RS18.13.378]

MELROSE, GEORGE, a feuar in Townhead of Duns, and his son Robert Melrose, a sasine, 1691. [NRS.RS18.5.177]

MELROSE, JOHN, in Paxton, testament, 1714. C.L. [NRS]

MELROSE, MATTHEW, in Townhead of Duns, a sasine, 1670. [NRS.RS18.2.234]

MELVILLE, GAVIN, a merchant in Coldstream, sasines, 1729-1757. [NRS.RS18.10.350; 13.520]

The People of the Scottish Borders, 1650-1800

MELVILLE, GEORGE, a merchant in Duns, a sasine, 1728, [NRS.RS18.10.268]; testament, 1738. C.L. [NRS]

MENEN, CULBERT, in Paxton, testament, 1683. C.L. [NRS]

MENNON, JOHN, portioner of Paxton, sasines, 1753-1763. [NRS.RS18.13.323; 14.442]

MENZIES, JOHN, a musician in Earlston, a sasine, 1768. [NRS.RS18.15.298]

MENZIES, MARJORIE, spouse to Patrick Gillespie in Symprin, testament, 1663. C.L. [NRS]

MERCER, ANDREW, in Lochbreast, Roxburghshire, portioner of Bridgend, heir to his grandfather Andrew Mercer a portioner there, 1799. [NRS.S/H]

MERCER, GEORGE, portioner of Darnick, a deed, 1756. [NRS.CC18.7.53]

MERCER, JAMES, in Newstead, a deed, 1759. [NRS.CC18.7.203]

MERCER, JOHN, in Roxburgh, a bond, 1760. [NRS.RD4.217.708]

MERCER, JOHN, a sergeant of the Royal Artillery at Woolwich, son and heir of John Mercer a weaver and portioner in Bridgend, 1792. [NRS.S/H]

MERCER, NINIAN, a writer in Coldstream, a sasine, 1688. [NRS.RS18.5.52]

MERCER, Dr ROBERT, in Selkirk, 1783. [NRS.E326.1.210]

MERTIN, ISOBEL, spouse of John Daill in Houndwood, testament, 1674. [C.L. [NRS]

MERTON, THOMAS, in Gattonside, deeds, 1758. [NRS.CC18.7.141/186]

METHVEN, JAMES, in Greenlaw, a sasine, 1678. [NRS.RS18.4.84]

METHVEN, WILLIAM, born 1644, minister at Fogo 1682-1689, died 14 April 1734. [F.2.16]

MIDDLEMISS, JAMES, jr., a farmer from Southcoat, Roxburghshire, was transported to the colonies in May 1726. [NRS.JC12.4]

The People of the Scottish Borders, 1650-1800

MIDDLEMISS, JAMES, sr., a farmer from Southcoat, Roxburghshire, was transported to the colonies in May 1726. [NRS.JC12.4]

MIDDLEMISS, THOMAS, in Paxton, sasines, 1733-1761. [NRS.RS18.11.99; 14.360]

MIDDLEMIST, AGNES, in Selkirk, 1783. [NRS.E326.1.210]

MIDDLEMIST, JANET, spouse to John Dickson in Dryburgh, testament, 1663. C.L. [NRS]

MILL, ALEXANDER, feuar in Coldstream, sasines, 1670-1683, [NRS.RS18.2.256; 4.244/400]; testament, 1688. C.L. [NRS]

MILL, CHARLES, a shoemaker in Duns, sasines, 1751-1759. [NRS.RS18.13.173/288; 14.77]

MILLER, GEORGE, in Ayton, testament, 1673. C.L. [NRS]

MILLER, GEORGE, a violer in Ayton, a sasine, 1715. [NRS.RS18.9.58]

MILLER, JAMES, a glazier in Duns, a sasine, 1711. [NRS.RS18.8.237]

MILLER, JAMES, a weaver in Earlston, testament, 1744. C.L. [NRS]

MILLER, JOHN, a physician in Kelso, sasines, 1765-1767. [NRS.RS18.15.76/286]

MILLER, NICOL, a herd in Houboig, a sasine, 1756. [NRS.RS18.13.516]

MILLER, PATRICK, a notary in Duns, a sasine, 1678. [NRS.RS18.4.89]

MILLER, THOMAS, born 1701, died 6 December 1778, his wife Isobel Trotter died 24 December 1763. [Abbey St Bathans MI, Berwickshire]

MILLER, WILLIAM, a thief and vagabond from Roxburghshire, was transported to the colonies in May 1731. [NRS.JC12.4]

MILLS, JOHN, a tenant in Darnchester, testament, 1759. C.L. [NRS]

MILNE, MARJORIE, in Bemersyde, spouse to Thomas Gardiner, testament, 1675. C.L. [NRS]

MINTO, WALTER, a vintner in Jedburgh, a deed, 1760. [NRS.CC18.7.295]

The People of the Scottish Borders, 1650-1800

MINTO, WILLIAM, a shoemaker in Duns, a sasine, 1728. [NRS.RS18.10.306]

MITCHELL, GUSTAVUS, a dyer in Hutton, sasines, 1762-1776. [NRS.RS18.14.394; 17.60]

MITCHELL, THOMAS, in Hunthall, testament, 1710. C.L. [NRS]

MITCHELL, WILLIAM, a skinner in Jedburgh, a deed, 1762. [NRS.CC18.7.386]

MITCHELLHILL, ALEXANDER, a skinner in Jedburgh, a deed, 1757. [NRS.CC18.7.94]

MITCHELLHILL, WILLIAM, in Camerlawes, testament, 1681. C.L. [NRS]

MOFFAT, ANDREW, born 1768, a baker in Duns, died 8 May 1845, his sons Alexander Moffat, born 1803, died in Charleston, South Carolina, on 17 September 1819, George Moffat, born 1800, died in Charleston, South Carolina, on 21 August 1844, and Andrew Moffat, born 1794, died on Sullivan's Island, South Carolina, on 22 August 1849. [Duns MI, Berwickshire]

MOFFAT, CHARLES, tenant in Lylston, testaments, 1734-1737. C.L. [NRS]

MOFFAT, HUGH, son of Alexander Moffat, a mason in West Reston, a sasine, 1752. [NRS.RS18.13.212]

MOFFAT, JOHN, of East Moristoun, born 1668, died 3 February 1743, husband of Sibella Hume. [Legerwood MI, Berwickshire]

MOFFAT, JOHN, late bailie of Lauder, testaments, 1743-1744. C.L. [NRS]

MOFFAT, JOHN, born 1719, died 23 October 1781, his spouse Margaret ..., born 1715, died 19 July 1811, their son John, born 1747, died 8 November 1829, his wife Jane Bogue, born 1758, died 22 April 1838. [Swinton MI]

MOFFAT, PATRICK, a weaver in Duns, a sasine, 1759. [NRS.RS18.14.79]

MOFFAT, WILLIAM, a burgess of Lauder, a sasine, 1780. [NRS.RS18.17.414]

MOIR, ANDREW, of Otterburn, a deed, 1761. [NRS.CC18.7.362]

MOIR, HENRY, a surgeon from Kelso, a Jacobite transported to the colonies in September 1748. [P.3.202]

The People of the Scottish Borders, 1650-1800

MOIR, JAMES, of Earnslaw, a sasine, 1753. [NRS.RS18.13.291]

MOIR, ROBERT, from Kelso, a Jacobite transported to the colonies in September 1748. [P.2.204]

MONCRIEFF, GEORGE, a gunsmith in Duns, and his son Andrew Moncrieff, a sasine, 1707. [NRS.RS18.7.344]

MONILAWS, JAMES, a merchant in Duns, a sasine, 1692. [NRS.RS18.5.220]

MONILAWS, JOHN, a feuar in Duns, testament, 1710. C.L. [NRS]

MONILAWS, PATRICK, of Duns Mylne, sasines, 1666-1669. [NRS.RS18.1.314; 2.179/190]

MONRO, JOHN, of Carrolside, a surgeon apothecary in Edinburgh, testament, 1740. C.L. [NRS]

MONTGOMERY, JAMES, of Stanhope, a sasine, 1778. [NRS.RS18.17.231]

MONTGOMERY, WILLIAM, of Whitslaid, testament, 1690. C.L. [NRS]

MOODIE, GEORGE, born 1645, minister at Fogo from 1693 until his death in 1721, spouse of Elizabeth Calderwood, [F.2.16]; testament, 1725. C.L. [NRS]

MOORE, ARCHIBALD, rentaler in Paxton, testament, 1679. C.L. [NRS]

MORISON, HENRY, of Hilton, a sasine, 1766. [NRS.RS18.15.183]

MOSCROP, JOHN, in Duns, sasines, 1681-1709. [NRS.RS18.4.236/469, etc]

MOSCROP, JOHN, town clerk of Duns, died 1695. [Duns MI, Berwickshire]

MOSCROP, ROBERT, a maltman in Duns, a sasine, 1701. [NRS.RS18.6.252]

MOSLEY, WILLIAM, born 1711, a wright in Coldstream, Berwickshire, died 3 June 1786, his spouse Elspeth Erskine, born 1712, died in February 1778. [Lennel MI, Berwickshire]

MOSSMAN, ADAM, portioner of Birgham, a sasine, 1665. [NRS.RS18.1.298]

MOSSMAN, WILLIAM, a maltman in Eyemouth, a sasine, 1716. [NRS.RS18.9.83]

The People of the Scottish Borders, 1650-1800

MOW, HENRY, a feuar in Coldstream, a sasine, 1754. [NRS.RS18.13.377]

MOWAT, JOSEPH, of Fawsyde, a sasine, 1677. [NRS.RS18.4.14]

MOWAT, WILLIAM, a maltman in Lauder, sasines, 1720. [NRS.RS18.9.381/395]

MUDIE, GEORGE, minister at Fogo, and his son Roger Mudie a student of divinity, sasines, 1723. [NRS.RS18.9.605/607]

MUIR, ARCHIBALD, portioner of Paxton, sasines, 1753-1779. [NRS.RS18.13.323, etc]

MUIR, GEORGE, in Coldingham, sasines, 1719-1743. [NRS.RS18.9.309/316]

MUIRHEAD, JAMES, of Breadisholm, a merchant in Lisbon, a sasine,1766. [NRS.RS18.15.224]

MURDOCH, PATRICK, in Blackadder Mill, a sasine, 1771. [NRS.RS18.16.64]

MURDOCH, PETER, in Wester Greenrigg, a sasine, 1780. [NRS.RS18.17.425]

MUREBURN, JAMES, in Eyemouth, a sasine, 1674. [NRS.RS18.3.196]

MURRAY, ADAM, minister at Abbey St Bathans from 1759 to 1774, minister at Eccles from 1774 until his death in 1797, husband of (1) Isobel Marshall, (2) Christian Bell[F.2.3/14]; a sasine, 1779. [NRS.RS18.17.364]

MURRAY, ALEXANDER, a bailie of Lauder, a sasine, 1721. [NRS.RS18.9.474]

MURRAY, ALEXANDER, son and heir of Lieutenant Colonel Walter Murray in Busch, Brabant, the Netherlands, 1669. [NRS.S/H]

MURRAY, ALEXANDER, son of Charles Murray clerk of the bailliary of Lauderdale, a merchant and naval officer in Charleston, South Carolina, before 1737. [NRS.S/H; RD3.210.491]

MURRAY, ARCHIBALD, a tailor in Denholm, deeds, 1760-1761. [NRS.CC18.7.297/305]

MURRAY, DAVID, son of John Murray of Philiphaugh, Selkirkshire, settled in Christchurch parish, Georgia, died in Savannah, Georgia, 29 April 1771, probate 17 February 1765, South Carolina. [AJ.1226]

The People of the Scottish Borders, 1650-1800

MURRAY, GEORGE, a cabinet-maker in Tweedmouth, a sasine, 1778. [NRS.RS18.17.194]

MURRAY, GEORGE, heir to his brother Patrick Murray who died 1 November 1780, in the lands and barony of Cherrytrees, parish of Yetholm, Roxburghshire, 1785. [NRS.S/H]

MURRAY, GILBERT, a messenger, a sasine, 1767. [NRS.RS18.15.261]

MURRAY, JAMES, educated at Glasgow University, minister at Yarrow from 1680 to 1691, father of Anne. [F.2.196]

MURRAY, JAMES, from Roxburghshire, a member of the Scots Charitable Society of Boston, 1765. [NEHGS]

MURRAY, JAMES, a dyer in Ednam, a sasine, 1777. [NRS.RS18.17.170]

MURRAY, JAMES, son of Gideon Murray of Sundhope, Selkirkshire, emigrated to Jamaica before 1766, settled at Airy Castle, St Thomas in the East. [NRS.RD2.236.634]

MURRAY, JOHN, in Coldstream, testament, 1684. C.L. [NRS]

MURRAY, JOHN, born 1705, a maltman in Longnewton, died 7 May 1741, father of David Murray, born 1737, died 26 December 1748. [Longnewton MI, Roxburghshire]

MURRAY, JOHN, a maltman in Selkirk, a deed, 1760. [NRS.CC18.7.233]

MURRAY, JOHN, from Philiphaugh, Selkirkshire, settled in Queen's County, Prince Edward Island, before 1769. [NRS.GD293.2.72]

MURRAY, JOHN, in Selkirk, 1783. [NRS.E326.1.210]

MURRAY, WALTER, a cooper in Melrose, a sasine, 1751. [NRS.RS18.13.109]

MUSCHET, DAVID, of Callzehatt, a sasine, 1674. [NRS.RS18.3.202]

NAPPER, JOSEPH, a baker and feuar in Kelso, eldest son of the late Robert Napper a baker and feuar there, heir to his grandfather Joseph Napper, a baker and feuar in Kelso, Roxburghshire, 1783. [SHR.37]

The People of the Scottish Borders, 1650-1800

NASMYTH, WILLIAM, educated at Edinburgh University, minister at Eckford from 1678 until 1689, died in Edinburgh 8 April 1696. [F.2.110]

NEILL, MARGARET, spouse to George Nisbet, testament, 1669. C.L. [NRS]

NEILL, ROBERT, a smith in Longformacus, his spouse Agnes Old, and their sons John Neill and Richard Neill, a sasine, 1766. [NRS.RS18..15.180]

NEILSON, WILLIAM, in West Gordon, testament, 1652. C.L. [NRS]

NEWTON, ANDREW, a merchant in Duns, a sasine, 1776. [NRS.RS18.17.24]

NEWTON, HENRY, a weaver in Bemersyde, testament, 1663. C.L. [NRS]

NEWTON, WILLIAM, a smith at Nisbet Pathhead, testament, 1787. C.L. [NRS]

NEWTON, Mrs, a shopkeeper in Kelso, 1785. [NRS.E326.4.1]

NICHOLSON, JOHN, a carpenter from Kelso, settled on Tortula before 1775. [NRS.RD2.236.499]

NICKLE, ROBERT, a shopkeeper in Kelso, 1785. [NRS.E326.4.1]

NICOL, JAMES, in Brieryhole, a deed, 1758. [NRS.CC18.7.178]

NICOL, JOHN, in Riccaltoun, a deed, 1756. [NRS.CC18.7.27]

NICOLL, MANIE, in Duns, testament, 1675. C.L. [NRS]

NICOLSON, ALEXANDER, minister at Bunkle from 1678 to 1690, died on Holy Island 1711, husband of Alison Hume, parents of Margaret, Elizabeth, and Janet. [F.2.5]

NICOLSON, PATRICK, a tailor in Wederly, testament, 1679. C.L. [NRS]

NICOLSON, THOMAS, in Wedderburn, testament, 1706. C.L. [NRS]

NICOLSON, WILLIAM, son of James Nicolson, gardener at Purves Hall, a sasine, 1707. [NRS.RS18.7.346]

NIER, WILLIAM, a merchant in Kelso, a deed, 1756. [NRS.CC18.7.29]

NISBET, BETTY, born 1750, spouse to Thomas Learmonth a wright in Clintmains, died 17 January 1790. [Earlston MI]

The People of the Scottish Borders, 1650-1800

NISBET, DAVID, a merchant in Eyemouth, a deed, 1756. [NRS.CC18.7.29]; a sasine, 1758, [LC#3204]; testaments, 1784-1788. C.L. [NRS]

NISBET, GILES, from Duns, Berwickshire, a cattle-thief transported to the colonies in September 1768. [AJ.1079]

NISBET, HARRY, in Paxton, testament, 1672. C.L. [NRS]

NISBET, JANET, from Duns, Berwickshire, a cattle-thief transported to the colonies in September 1768. [AJ.1079]

NISBET, JOHN, a cordiner in Coldingham, a sasine, 1664. [NRS.RS18.1.245]

NISBET, JOHN, a merchant in Eyemouth, a sasine, 1758. [LC#3204]

NISBET, PATRICK, a maltman in Duns, sasines, 1726-1754. [NRS.RS18.12.383/385; 13.365]

NISBET, WILLIAM, a clothier in Duns, a sasine, 1696. [NRS.RS18.5.328]

NISBET, WILLIAM, a merchant in Eyemouth, a sasine, 1758. [LC#3204]; testament, 1774. C.L. [NRS]

NIVEN, JOHN, portioner of Whitsome, a sasine, 1752. [NRS.RS18.13.255]

NIXON, JOHN, a shopkeeper in Hawick, 1785. [NRS.E326.4.1]

NOBLE, JAMES, minister at Eckfoord, a sasine, 1707. [NRS.RS18.7.230]

NOTMAN, DAVID, a mason in Mellerstain, testament, 1770. C.L. [NRS]

NOTMAN, JOHN, a fiddler in Swinton, sasines. 1753-1778. [NRS.RS18.13.264/346; 14.83/92/249, etc]

NUTTER, JAMES, from Jedburgh, a thief and housebreaker, who was transported to the colonies in June 1771. [NRS.RH2.4.255]

OGG, WILLIAM, born 1735, Excise Supervisor at Duns, died 18 July 1818, his spouse Elisabeth Paterson, born 1778, died 24 July 1844. [Duns MI]

OGILL, WILLIAM, of Popill Hall, a sasine, 1717. [NRS.RS18.9.157]

OGILVIE, ALEXANDER, in Gorrenberry, a deed, 1760. [NRS.CC18.7.266]

The People of the Scottish Borders, 1650-1800

OGILVIE, CHRISTIAN, heir to his deceased husband Thomas Robertson, gardener and feuar in Kelso, 1770. [SHR.31]

OGILVIE, JANE, relict of Thomas Monilaws a carrier in Duns, testament, 1729. C.L. [NRS]

OGILVIE, WILLIAM, of Harwoodmyres, a deed of factory, 1759. [NRS.CC18.7.230]

OLD, THOMAS, minister at Ligertwood, testaments, 1740-1750. C.L. [NRS]

OLD, WILLIAM, a cooper in Coldstream, testament, 1752. C.L. [NRS]

OLIVER, ADAM, a gardener in Hunthill, a deed, 1758. [NRS.CC18.7.164]

OLIVER, ADAM, a slater in Jedburgh, a deed, 1758. [NRS.CC18.7.164]

OLIVER, ALEXANDER, in Hershope, a deed, 1757. [NRS.CC18.7.109]

OLIVER, ALEXANDER or DAN, in Westshiels, a deed, 1756. [NRS.CC18.7.20]

OLIVER, ANDREW, a flesher in Jedburgh, deeds, 1756-1759. [NRS.CC18.7.24/37/203]

OLIVER, DAVID, in Westshiells, a deed, 1757. [NRS.CC18.7.56]

OLIVER, or FISHER, ELIZABETH, in Jedburgh, a deed, 1756. [NRS.CC18.7.49]

OLIVER, GEORGE, a thatcher in Jedburgh, a deed, 1758. [NRS.CC18.7.164]

OLIVER, GILBERT, in Dykeraw, a deed, 1758. [NRS.CC18.7.149]

OLIVER, JAMES, from Jedburgh, a Covenanter who was transported from Leith to Jamaica in August 1685, landed at Port Royal, Jamaica. [RPCS.II.329][LC175]

OLIVER, JAMES, a shopkeeper in Hawick, 1785. [NRS.E326.4.1]

OLIVER, JAMES, born 1774 in Berwick-on-Tweed, a planter, married ..... Meldrum in Berwick-on-Tweed in November 1804, died in Savanna, Georgia, on 26 May 1808. [Savanna Republican, 28 May 1808][SM.66/971; 70/719] [Savanna Death Register]

OLIVER, JOHN, a butcher in Jedburgh, deeds, 1759-1760. [NRS.CC18.7.197/279]

OLIVER, JOHN, a shoemaker in Hawick, a deed, 1758. [NRS.CC18.7.167]

OLIVER, PATRICK, in Hindles, a deed, 1757. [NRS.CC18.7.69]

OLIVER, ROBERT, in Ainslie, a contract, 1760. [NRS.CC18.7.234]

OLIVER, ROBERT, a merchant in Jedburgh, deeds, 1756. [NRS.CC18.7.38/49]

OLIVER, STEPHEN, in Woodhouse, a deed, 1758. [NRS.CC18.7.173]

OLIVER, THOMAS, in Gladstains, a tack, 1758. [NRS.CC18.7.187]

OLIVER, THOMAS, in Jedburgh, a deed, 1760. [NRS.CC18.7.279]

OLIVER, THOMAS, in Longrow, a deed, 1757. [NRS.CC18.7.68]

OLIVER, THOMAS, in Westerhouses, a deed, 1756. [NRS.CC18.7.37]

OLIVER, THOMAS, born 1745 [possibly son of Thomas Oliver a nailer in Denholm, Roxburghshire], a blacksmith and indentured servant, with wife and two children, emigrated via Whitby to Savannah, Georgia, aboard the Marlborough in August 1774. [TNA.T47.9/11]

OLIVER, WILLIAM, in Longrow, a deed, 1759. [NRS.CC18.7.204]

OLIVER, WILLIAM, a shopkeeper in Hawick, 1785. [NRS.E326.4.1]

ORANGE, WILLIAM, a dishmaker in Cockburnspath, and his wife Magdalen Grieve, a sasine, 1748. [NRS.RS18.12.406]

ORMISTON, CHARLES, born 1625, a merchant in Kelso, a Quaker 1665, husband of Janet Chatto. [NRS.Scottish Quaker Records, k17.86]

ORMSTON, JAMES, a merchant in Kelso, eldest son of James Ormston, a barber and innkeeper there, heir to his uncle Charles Ormston, a skinner in Kelso, 1790. [NRS.S/H]; a shopkeeper in Kelso, 1785. [NRS.E326.4.1]

ORMSTON, JANE, wife of John Waldie, writer in Kelso, heir to her brother William Ormston, M.D. in Kelso who died 16 December 1770, 1771. [NRS.S/H]

The People of the Scottish Borders, 1650-1800

ORMSTON, JOHN, shoemaker in Kelso, died 5 January 1745, his spouse Sophia Mills died 20 February 1795. [Kelso MI]

ORROCK, ALEXANDER, born 1652, son of Alexander Orrock of Orrock and his wife Elizabeth Wemyss, minister at Hawick 1691 until his death on 23 April 1711. [F.2.114]

OSWALD, JAMES, a notary in Coldstream, testament, 1665. C.L. [NRS]

OURD, WILLIAM, servant to James Waugh tenant in Ligertwood, testament, 1741. C.L. [NRS]

OVENS, BARBARA, in Windpath, testament, 1760. C.L. [NRS]

PAE, ALEXANDER, a writer in Eyemouth, and his spouse Beatrix Dickson, a sasine, 1674. [NRS.RS18.3.228]

PAE, GEORGE, a weaver in Coldingham, sasine, 1690. [NRS.RS18.5.141]

PAITSON, JAMES, in Westruther, testament, 1663. C.L. [NRS]

PALLEIN, JOHN, in Lendilhill, testament, 1655. C.L. [NRS]

PALMER, JAMES, a printer and merchant in Kelso, Roxburghshire, 1785, [NRS.E326.4.1]; 1798. [NRS.CS97.112.98]

PANTON, GEORGE ANN, in Kelso, sasines, 1777. [NRS.RS18.17.113/148]

PANTON, Reverend GEORGE, formerly in Shelbourne, Nova Scotia, and New York, lately in Kelso, Roxburghshire, probate October 1810, PCC.

PANTON, JAMES, a smith in Coldstream, sasines, 1775-1777. [NRS.RS18.16.431/439; 17.180]

PARK, EBENEZER, a joiner in Coldstream, a sasine, 1770. [NRS.RS18.15.471]

PARK, GEORGE, in Coldingham, sasines, 1667-1704. [NRS.RS18.2.27; 3.402; 6.360/507/510]

PARK, ISOBEL, eldest sister of Alexander Park a cooper in Hutton, testament, 1748. C.L. [NRS]

The People of the Scottish Borders, 1650-1800

PARK, JOHN, born 1708, a schoolmaster from Horndean, Ladykirk, Berwickshire, emigrated via London in November 1736. [CLRO/AIA]

PARK, MUNGO, the elder, in Redpath Milne, testament, 1727. C.L. [NRS]

PARK, MUNGO, born 1701, a wright in Earlston, died 29 December 1751. [Earlston MI]

PARK, ROBERT, minister at Foulden, testament, 1759. C.L. [NRS]

PARK, THOMAS, a cooper in Hutton, a sasine, 1764. [NRS.RS18.15.9]

PARROTT, JAMES, a farrier in Ayton, sasines, 1775-1776. [NRS,RS18.15.86; 17.47/100]

PATERSON, ALEXANDER, a fisher in Eyemouth, a sasine, 1776. [NRS.RS18.16.451]

PATERSON, ANDREW, a minister at Whitsome, a sasine 1666. [NRS.RS18.1.315]

PATTERSON, GEORGE, portioner of Midlem, a deed, 1759. [NRS.CC18.7.198]

PATERSON, JAMES, a mason in Earlston, a sasine, 1708. [NRS.RS18.9.475]

PATTERSON, JAMES, portioner in Bowden, son and heir of Robert Patterson portioner there, 1796. [NRS.S/H]

PATERSON, Sir JOHN, of Eccles, testament, 1782. C.L. [NRS]

PATTERSON, JOHN, portioner of Midlem, deeds, 1758-1759. [NRS.CC18.7.131/198]

PATTERSON, JOHN, born 1768, weaver in Kirkgate, Earlston, died 20 January 1797, husband of Elizabeth Pringle, born 1767, died 26 July 1799. [Earlston MI]

PATERSON, PATRICK, a merchant in Duns, a sasine, 1662. [NRS.RS18.1.29]

PATERSON, ROBERT, in Muirhouselaw, a deed, 1760. [NRS.CC18.7.260]

PATTERSON, THOMAS, portioner of Midlem, deeds, 1758-1759. [NRS.CC18.7.131/198]

The People of the Scottish Borders, 1650-1800

PATERSON, WILLIAM, a wright in Coldingham, a sasine, 1776. [NRS.RS18.17.46]

PATOUN, MICHAEL, in Eyemouth, testament, 1691. C.L. [NRS]

PATOUN, WALTER, a smith in Harklie Loanen, afterwards in Coldstream, a sasine, 1774. [NRS.RS18.16.346]

PAXTON, DAVID, of West Reston, sasines, 1659. [NRS.RS18.4.78/83]

PAXTON, JAMES, in Edincraw, testament, 1676. C.L. [NRS]

PAXTON, JOHN, born 1729, died 18 June 1804, his spouse Agnes Bowmaker, born 1742, died 10 August 1814. [Chirnside MI, Berwickshire]

PAXTON, LANCELOT, portioner of Auchincraw, a sasine, 1701. [NRS.RS18.6.243]

PEACE, JEAN, spouse to John Cockburn, in Coatrig, testament, 1676. C.L. [NRS]

PEACOCK, AGNES, in Westruther, testament, 1652. C.L. [NRS]

PEARSON, JAMES, a smith in Hutton, testament, 1750. C.L. [NRS]

PEARSON, JOHN, of Kippenross, sasines, 1679-1700. [NRS.RS18.4.151/280,etc]

PEARSON, KATHERINE, relict of Thomas Nisbet in Paxton, testament, 1717. C.L. [NRS]

PEARSON, THOMAS, a notary public in Nenthorne, a sasine, 1659. [NRS.RS18.4.47]

PEATSON, ANDREW, a mason in Newtown of Coldstream, a sasine, 1701. [NRS.RS18.6.193]

PEATTIE, JEAN, relict of John Paxton in Coldingham, testament, 1777. C.L. [NRS]

PENCE, MARGARET, spouse to William Home in Chirnside, testament, 1669. C.L. [NRS]

PENMAN, JANET, spouse of William Marjoribanks, testament, 1654. C.L. [NRS]

The People of the Scottish Borders, 1650-1800

PENNIE, ISOBEL, spouse of Ralph Smith in Chirnside, testament, 1683. C.L. [NRS]

PENNY, ROBERT, in Earnslaw, a sasine, 1712. [NRS.RS18.8.372]

PENNYCOOK, JAMES, born 1669, died 6 December 1727, his wife Mary, born 1741, died July 1801. [Ayton MI, Berwickshire]

PENTLAND, WILLIAM, in Foulden, testament, 1683. C.L. [NRS]

PETER, JAMES, of Chapel, testament, 1695. C.L. [NRS]

PETER, WALTER, of Chappell, sasines, 1770-1776. [NRS.RS18.16.2/5; 17.15]

PHILIP, ROBERT, tenant in Swinewood Mill, testament, 1780. C.L. [NRS]

PILMUIR, JOHN, in Fishwick, sasine, 1755. [NRS.RS18.13.464]

PINKERTON, OSOBEL, spouse of Ninian Bell in Eccles, testament, 1665. C.L. [NRS]

PIRIE, ISOBEL, spouse of James Golightlie in Howbooge, testament, 1669. C.L. [NRS]

PITT, ANDREW, born 1704, died at Greenend 22 December 1791. [Ancrum MI]

PLENDERLEITH, ISOBEL, spouse to George Samson in Lidgertwood, testament, 1663. C.L. [NRS]

PLUMMER, ROBERT, son of Andrew Plummer of Middlestead, a sasine, 1695. [NRS.RS18.5.287]

POLWORTH, ALEXANDER, a smith in Coldcrooks, a sasine, 1711. [NRS.RS18.8.253]

POLWART, WILLIAM, a wright in Coldham, testament, 1663. C.L. [NRS]

POOGS, GEORGE, minister at Cockburnspath, testament, 1671. C.L. [NRS]

PORTEOUS, JOHN, in Duns, a sasine, 1770. [NRS.RS18.15.430]

PORTER, MATTHEW, born 1719, feuar in Ayton, died 8 July 1791, his spouse Margaret Crosbie, born 1727, died 6 November 1781. [Coldingham MI]; sasine, 1768. [NRS.RS18.15.335]

POTTS, ANDREW, a writer in Kelso, sasines, 1765-1773. [NRS.RS18.15.142; 16.230]

POTT, ANTHONY, from Jedburgh, was transported from Leith to Barbados on 17 April 1666. [Edinburrgh Tolbooth Records.106]

POTT, HELEN, born 1757, spouse to Robert Stavert, died 2 December 1784. [Cavers MI]

POTTS, JAMES, heir to his father Andrew Potts, writer in Kelso, 1770. [NRS.S/H]

POTTS, WILLIAM, in Dernchester, sasines, 1775. [NRS.RS18.16.392/431/439]

POW, JAMES, in Eyemouth, a sasine, 1755. [NRS.RS18.13.442]

POW, JOHN, a minister at Coldstream, testament, 1735. C.L. [NRS]

POW, WILLIAM, a merchant in Eyemouth, formerly a merchant and bailie of Coldstream, a sasine, 1744. [NRS.RS18.12.75]

POWRIE, WILLIAM, son of Richard Powrie in Dawyck, Peebles-shire, settled in Barbados as a planter before 1630, died there 1648, probate 1649, Barbados; probate 1651 PCC. [EBR.44.1912; 25.1086][NRS.GD34.932]

PRINGLE, ADAM, a clockmaker in Edinburgh, heir to his brother Andrew Pringle a wright in Mellerstaine, 1790. [NRS.S/H]

PRINGLE, ALEXANDER, a surgeon in Kelso, sasines, 1673-1703. [NRS.RS18.3.66; 6.420]

PRINGLE, FRANCIS, in Selkirk, 1783. [NRS.E326.1.210]

PRINGLE, GEORGE, bailie of Kelso, a sasine, 1703. [NRS.RS18.6.420]

PRINGLE, GEORGE, portioner of Earlston, testament, 1722. C.L. [NRS]

PRINGLE, GEORGE, mealmaker in Lauder, testament, 1752. C.L. [NRS]

The People of the Scottish Borders, 1650-1800

PRINGLE, JAMES, from Teviotdale, a member of the Scots Charitable Society of Boston, 1753. [NEHGS]

PRINGLE, JAMES, a weaver in Coldstream, sasines, 1773-1774. [NRS.RS18.16.291/346]

PRINGLE, JOHN, born 1628, son of George Pringle of Balmungo a major in the service of Gustavus Adolphus of Sweden, minister at Fogo 1660 until his death in 1664, spouse of Jean Shaw. [F.2.15]

PRINGLE, JOHN, from the Merse, Berwickshire, a member of the Scots Charitable Society of Boston, 1739. [NEHGS]

PRINGLE, JOHN, a merchant in Madeira, second son of the late John Pringle of Haining, was granted Haining on 10 December 1754. [NRS.RGS.103.62]

PRINGLE, ROBERT, a merchant in Home, testament, 1731. C.L. [NRS]

PRINGLE, ROBERT, son of John Pringle of Haining, a physician in Jamaica, died in Philadelphia on 13 October 1775. [SM.38.53]

PRINGLE, WALTER, a surgeon apothecary in Earlston, sasines, 1703-1705. [NRS.RS18.6.469; 7.105]

PRINGLE, WILLIAM, born 1680, gardener in Dryburgh, died 2 February 1745, his spouse Agnes Culdilock, born 1680, died 9 July 1755. [Dryburgh Abbey MI]

PUMPHRIE, Captain CHRISTOPHER, of Berriehaugh, a sasine, 1723. [NRS.RS18.9.588]

PURDIE, JOHN, a farmer in Paxton, testament, 1699. C.L. [NRS]

PURDIE, WILLIAM, a shoemaker in Paxton, sasines, 1770-1772. [NRS.RS18.15.466; 16.159]

PURDOM, WALTER, in Hawick, a deed, 1758. [NRS.CC18.7.179]

PURVES, AGNES, born 1739, died 1816. [Abbey St Bathans MI, Berwickshire]

PURVES, ARCHIBALD, wright in Eyemouth, sasine, 1751. [NRS.RS18.13.144]

The People of the Scottish Borders, 1650-1800

PURVES, ARCHIBALD, in Fishwick, testament, 1775. C.L. [NRS]

PURVES, GEORGE, born 1716, a vintner in Duns, sasines 1752-1775, [NRS.RS18.13.249/268; 16.389]; died 19 April 1791. [Duns MI]

PURVES, JOHN, born 1721, died 9 August 1761. [Mindrum MI]

PURVES, JOHN HOME, baptised 25 January 1784 in Hutton, Berwickshire, eldest son of Sir Alexander Purves of Purves Hall, Berwickshire, HM Consul in Pensacola, West Florida, died there 20 September 1827. [Hutton OPR] [GM.97/573][BM.23/270] [AJ.4172][EEC.18146]

PURVES, JOSEPH, a mason in Eyemouth, sasines, 1750-1779. [NRS.RS18.13.42/214/490; 17.392]

PURVES, PATRICK, a merchant in Eyemouth, testament, 1797. C.L. [NRS]; born 1720, died 9 February 1797, husband of Isobel Binnie, born 1719, died 10 July 1796. [Coldingham MI, Berwickshire]

PURVES, THOMAS, born 1699, feuar in Coldingham, died 6 February 1779, his spouse Janet Rymer, died 14 September 1793. [Coldingham MI]

PURVES, Sir WILLIAM, of that Ilk, testaments, 1704-1705. C.L. [NRS]

QUARRIE, WILLIAM, in Crailinghall, a deed, 1757. [NRS.CC18.7.62]

RAE, GEORGE, a maltman in Duns, a sasine, 1701. [NRS.RS18.6.260]

RAE, JAMES, in Dalcove, testament, 1668. C.L. [NRS]

RAE, MARGARET, in Kelso, daughter and heir of Thomas Rae a feuar in Kelso, 1795. [NRS.S/H]

RAE, THOMAS, born 1723, a feuar in Kelso, died 18 March 1795, husband of Isabella Pringle, born 1744, died 12 September 1782. [Kelso MI]

RAEBURN, ..., a merchant in Kelso, a Quaker, 1666. [RPCS.3.11.135]

RAIT, JOHN, at Coldstream, testament, 1777. C.L. [NRS]

RAIT, THOMAS, of Longformacus, sasines, 1766-1777. [NRS.RS18.15.224.etc]

RAITH, JAMES, burgess of Lauder, sasines, 1775-1776. [NRS.RS18.16.407,etc]

The People of the Scottish Borders, 1650-1800

RALPH, GEORGE, a maltster and feuar in Duns, a sasine, 1766, [NRS.RS18.15.179]; testament, 1768. C.L. [NRS]

RAMSAY, ALEXANDER, son of John Ramsay, a tobacconist in Duns, a sasine, 1750. [NRS.RS18.13.23]

RAMSAY, GEORGE, of Edington, sasines, 1674-1700. [NRS.RS18.3.181; 6.127]

RAMSAY, GILBERT, bailie of Kelso, 1739. [NRS.CS228.B.2. 95]

RAMSAY, JAMES, born 1672, minister at Eyemouth, 1693-1707, at Kelso from 1707 until his death on 3 July 1749, husband of (1) Alison Nisbet, (2) Margaret Borthwick, father of Jean and Elizabeth. [F.2.72]

RAMSAY, JOHN, of Nunlands, testament, 1701. C.L. [NRS]

RAMSAY, JOHN, a tobacconist afterwards a candlemaker in Kelso, a sasine, 1772. [NRS.RS18.16.210]

RANKINE, ALEXANDER, in Greenlaw, sasines, 1754-1779. [NRS.RS18.13.377; 17.345/361]

RANKINE, GEORGE, in Oxmuir, testament, 1709. C.L. [NRS]

RANKINE, WILLIAM, in Eccles, sasines, 1710-1714, [NRS.RS18.8.172/473]; testament, 1733. C.L. [NRS]

RANDALL, JEAN, in Kelso, heir to her father William Randall there, 1789. [NRS.S/H]

REA, JAMES, born 1679, died 16 April 1719, his spouse Mary, died 18 November 1739. [Mindrum MI]

REA, JOHN, born 1680, died 6 November 1740. [Mindrum MI]

REDFORD, ANDREW, in Midlem, died 1685. [NRS.Scottish Quaker Records, k17.87/118]

REDFORD, THOMAS, a Quaker in Kelso, father of Samuel born 1674, possibly the Thomas Redford, an indentured servant shipped to East New Jersey in 1684. [NRS.SQR.K17][NJSA.EJD.A]

The People of the Scottish Borders, 1650-1800

REDFORD, WILLIAM, born in Friarshaw, Teviotdale, 1642, possibly the William Redford a Quaker in Barlands, Kelso, 1670s, an indentured servant, to East New Jersey 1682, settled in Essex County, East New Jersey, 1692, died 1725. [NJSA.EJD.A114.D][NRS.SQR.K17]

REDIE, MARGARET, in Bowen, testament, 1670. C.L. [NRS]

REDPATH, ANDREW, son of Patrick Redpath in Byrecleuch, a sasine, 1671. [NRS.RS18.2.351]

REDPATH, GEORGE, minister at Ladykirk, testament, 1741. C.L. [NRS]

REDPATH, GEORGE, innkeeper in Berwick, a sasine, 1775. [NRS.RS18.16.400]

REDPATH, JOSEPH, of Angelraw, sasines, 1759. [NRS.RS18.14.126/135/136/138/143]

REDPATH, MARGARET, relict of Alexander Hunter a merchant in Duns, testament, 1759. C.L. [NRS]

REDPATH, ROBERT, the younger, a butcher in Duns, testament, 1728. C.L. [NRS]

REDPATH, WILLIAM, a merchant in Duns, sasines, 1750-1772. [NRS.RS18.13.1/113/143/201; 16.141]

REID, CHRISTIAN, a silversmith in Newcastle, eldest son of Andrew Reid a brewer in Canongate, heir to his cousin Robert Kerr of Hoselaw, son of Robert Kerr of Hoselaw, 1793. [NRS.S/H]

REID, JAMES, a feuar in Duns, sasines, 1758-1760. [NRS.RS18..13.541; 14.175]

REID, JOHN, born 1715, herd in Hathornside, died 1 May 1772, father of James Reid, born 1750, herd in Southdean, died 11 February 1800. [Cavers MI]

REID, JOHN, in Lochburnfoot, a deed, 1758. [NRS.CC18.7.136]

REID, JOHN, a gardener in Kelso, a contract, 1757. [NRS.CC18.7.87]

REID, PATRICK, brother of Robert Reid, a merchant in Duns, a sasine, 1706. [NRS.RS18.7.159]

The People of the Scottish Borders, 1650-1800

REID, WALTER, born 1698, tenant in Ormiston, died 15 October 1748, his spouse Barbara Stavert, born 1704, died 1 April 1777. [Cavers MI]

REID, WILLIAM, in Whithope, deeds, 1760. [NRS.CC18.7.242/243]

REID, WILLIAM, a shoemaker in Jedburgh, a deed, 1756. [NRS.CC16.7.29]

RENNICK, THOMAS, a tailor in Askirkmiln, a deed, 1761. [NRS.CC18.7.305]

RENTON, ALEXANDER, of Lamberton, sasines, 1774-1780. [NRS.RS18.16.349/393/394; 17.426]

RENTON, DAVID, a drover in Duns, a sasine, 1728. [NRS.RS18.10.286]

RENTON, GEORGE, a drover in Fogo, testament, 1727. C.L. [NRS]

RENTON, JAMES, a writer in Eyemouth, sasines, 1697-1698, [NRS.RS18.5.338/376]; testament, 1751. C.L. [NRS]

RENTON, JOHN, son of the late John Renton of Lamerton, Berwickshire, 1654. [RGS.X.365]

RENTON, JOHN, of Lamberton, testament, 1776. C.L. [NRS]

RENTON, Captain WILLIAM, a merchant in Eyemouth, a sasine, 1778. [NRS.RS18.17.222]

RENWICK, WILLIAM, a plasterer in Berwick, sasines, 1767. [NRS.RS18.15.256/265]

RENWICK, WILLIAM, born in Roxburghshire, husband of Jane Jeffrey, settled in New York during 1794, a merchant there. [St Andrew's Society of NY.II.25]

RESTON, ALEXANDER, portioner of Hutton, sasines, 1702. [NRS.RS18.6.327/341/343/363]

RESTON, JAMES, son of James Reston the elder, portioner of Hutton, a sasine, 1674. [NRS.RS18.3.241]

RICHARDSON, ANDREW, in Maxton, a deed, 1758. [NRS.CC18.7.142]

RICHARDSON, DAVID, servant and grieve to Alexander Hay of Drumelzeer, testament, 1761. C.L. [NRS]

The People of the Scottish Borders, 1650-1800

RICHARDSON, GEORGE, born 1710, of Learmouth Mill, died 27 May 1760, his spouse Isobel, born 1713, died 1 July 1782, and daughter Gaeni Bell, born 1740, died 3 June 1769. [Mindrum MI]

RICHARDSON, Sir JOHN, of Smettoun, the elder, asasine, 1677. [NRS.RS18.4.2]

RICHARDSON, JOHN, in Tordoff, a deed, 1761. [NRS.CC18.7.341]

RICHARDSON, JOHN, a merchant and saddler in Kelso, sasines, 1753-1754. [NRS.RS18.13.305/396]

RICHARDSON, PATRICK, in Coldingham, sasines, 1755-1771. [NRS.RS18.13.451/548; 16.123]

RICHARDSON, THOMAS, a gardener in Eyemouth, a sasine, 1760. [NRS.RS18.14.247]

RICHARDSON, WILLIAM, a saddler in Kelso, a deed, 1761. [NRS.CC18.7.338]

RICHIE, CHRISTIAN, in Newton, a deed, 1757. [NRS.CC18.7.118]

RICHIESON, JAMES, in Kirklands, a deed, 1761. [NRS.CC18.7.382]

RICKLINGTON, WILLIAM, a gardener in Ayton, his spouse Jean Orkney, and their son John Ricklington, a sasine, 1772. [NRS.RS18.16.175]

RIDDELL, GEORGE, a gardener in Melkington, a deed, 1760. [NRS.CC18.7.277]

RIDDELL, JAMES, in Lauder, testament, 1758. C.L. [NRS]

RIDDELL, JOHN, in Pinnacle, a deed, 1760. [NRS.CC18.7.275]

RIDDELL, JOHN, portioner of Maxton, a deed, 1760. [NRS.CC18.7.277]

RIDDELL, PATRICK, of St Boswells, a sasine, 1746. [NRS.RS18.12.299]

RIDDELL, ROBERT, youngest son of Sir Walter Riddell of that Ilk, minister at Lilliesleaf from 1737 until his death on 12 March 1760; husband of Esther Riddell. [F.2.183]

RIDDEL, ROBERT, in Longnewton, father of Janet died 14 August 1732 aged 9. [Longnewton MI, Roxburghshire]

RIDDELL, ROBERT, in Biddletonhill, a deed, 1760. [NRS.CC18.7.277]

RIDDELL, ROBERT, in Bosiden, a deed, 1762. [NRS.CC18.7.384]

RIDDELL, ROBERT, in Middleton, deeds, 1759. [NRS.CC18.7.214/218]

RIDDELL, WALTER, in Abbotsrule Miln, a deed, 1761. [NRS.CC18.7.377]

RIDDELL, WILLIAM, a merchant in Berwick, sasines, 1773-1778. [NRS.RS18.16.281/333; 17.130/174/239]

RIDDELL, WILLIAM, in Selkirk, 1783. [NRS.E326.1.210]

RIDEPATH, THOMAS, born 1719, a shepherd in Flemington, died 7 July 1795, his spouse Betty, born 1736, died 13 April 1807. [Ayton MI, Berwickshire]

RITCHIE, GEORGE, in Mungowalls, testament, 1727. C.L. [NRS]

RITCHIE, JOHN, a gardener at Coldingham, testament, 1748. C.L. [NRS]

ROBERTSON, ABRAHAM, a clothier in Lintlaws, a sasine, 1734. [NRS.RS18.11.161]

ROBERTSON, ADAM, in Eyemouth, sasines, 1658. [NRS.RS18.4.16/17/18]

ROBERTSON, ALEXANDER, a maltman and feuar in Eyemouth, sasines, 1680-1712, [NRS.RS18.4.202/223/; 5.55; 8.295]; testament, 1716. C.L. [NRS]

ROBERTSON, ANDREW, a Lieutenant of the 58th Regiment of Foot, heir to his father Andrew Robertson or Robinson, sometime in Calcutta, afterwards a merchant in Kelso, 1789. [NRS.S/H]

ROBERTSON, ARCHIBALD, son of Patrick Robertson, vicar of Berwick, a sasine, 1719. [NRS.RS18.9.352]

ROBERTSON, DAVID, a merchant in Kelso, a sasine, 1750. [NRS.RS18.13.46]

ROBERTSON, ESTER, daughter of Thomas Robertson in Bridgend of Kelso, 1699, Quakers. [NRS.SQR.E15/96]

ROBERTSON, JAMES, a shoemaker in Eyemouth, a sasine, 1681. [NRS.RS18..4.263]

The People of the Scottish Borders, 1650-1800

ROBERTSON, JOHN, a joiner in Berwick, a sasine, 1773. [NRS.RS18.16.245]

ROBERTSON, MARGARET, from Jedburgh, a gypsy transported from Glasgow to Virginia on 1 January 1715. [GR.530]

ROBERTSON, MARION, relict of William Bookless in Eyemouth, testament, 1749. C.L. [NRS]

ROBERTSON, PATRICK, vicar of Berwick, a sasine, 1691. [NRS.RS18.5.169]

ROBERTSON, ROBERT, of Prenderguest, a merchant in Eyemouth, sasines, 1764-1769. [NRS.RS18.15.46/318/377/378]

ROBERTSON, SAMUEL, a brewer and Quaker in Ednam, born 1750, died 1807, his spouse Margaret Robertson, born 1760, died 1826. [Ednam MI]

ROBERTSON, THOMAS, gardener at the Bridgend of Kelso, husband of Margaret Hanna, 1670. [NRS.SQR, k17.86/118/119]

ROBERTSON, THOMAS, born 1736, minister at Selkirk from 1772 until his death on 5 September 1805; husband of Robina Lang. [F.2.195]

ROBERTSON, WILLIAM, a mason in Berwick, sasines, 1724-1725. [NRS.RS18.10.1/3/4/24/81]

ROBERTSON, WILLIAM, a merchant in Eyemouth, testaments, 1738/1741. C.L. [NRS]

ROBINSON, ARCHIBALD, born 1689, died 3 September 1712. [Cavers MI]

ROBINSON, JAMES, a wright in Cavers, spouse of Christian Lamb, born 1688, died 22 September 1725. [Cavers MI]

ROBISON, ANDREW, a prisoner in Duns Tolbooth, transferred to Edinburgh Tolbooth, 1663, a Quaker. [NRS.Edinburgh Tolbooth Register] [RPCS.3.II.105/135]

ROBSON, ANDREW, convenor of the Trades of Jedburgh, deeds, 1756-1759. [NRS.CC18.7.34/228]; heir to his father Adam Robson, late Convenor of the Trades of Jedburgh, 1763. [SHR.28]

ROBSON, ANDREW, flesher in Jedburgh, a deed, 1757. [NRS.CC18.7.116]

The People of the Scottish Borders, 1650-1800

ROBSON, ELIZABETH, in Jedburgh, a deed, 1756. [NRS.CC18.7.34]

ROBSON, GEORGE, a gardener at Jedburgh Milne, a deed, 1759. [NRS.CC18.7.210]

ROBSON, JAMES, a merchant in Jedburgh, deeds, 1756-1761. [NRS.CC18.7.13/21/352]

ROBSON, WILLIAM, in Hawkeep, a deed, 1761. [NRS.CC18.7.378]

ROBSON, WILLIAM, Provost of Jedburgh, a deed, 1756. [NRS.CC18.7.34]

ROCHEAD, GEORGE, in Cockburnspath, testament, 1669. C.L. [NRS]

ROCHEAD, JOHN, in Fogo Miln, testament, 1711. C.L. [NRS]

RODGER, ISOBEL, spouse of John Bichet in West Gordon, testament, 1680. C.L. [NRS]

RODGER, JAMES, in Selkirk, 1783. [NRS.E326.1.210]

RODGER, Major SAMUEL, in Berwick, sasines, 1758-1760. [NRS.RS18.13.567; 14.215]

ROMANES, JOHN, a merchant in Lauder, a sasine, 1775. [NRS.RS18.16.386]

ROMANES, ROBERT, a shoemaker burgess of Lauder, sasines, 1765-1779, [NRS.RS18.15.121/122; 16.386; 17.295]; testament, 1771. C.L. [NRS]

ROMANES, SIMON, born at Raecleugh, Westruther, 21 April 1750, died in Kelso 1803. [Kelso MI]

ROMANES, WILLIAM, a cordiner in Lauder, testament, 1677. C.L. [NRS]

ROME, JOHN, in Longlands, a deed, 1760. [NRS.CC18.7.299]

ROSS, JEAN, from Jedburgh, a gypsy who was transported from Glasgow to Virginia on 1 January 1715. [GR.530]

ROTHIE, GEORGE, in Lilliesleaf, a deed, 1757. [NRS.CC18.7.95]

ROTHIE, WILLIAM, in Lilliesleaf, deeds, 1757. [NRS.CC18.7.95/100]

The People of the Scottish Borders, 1650-1800

ROUGHEAD, WILLIAM, a mason in Berwick, sasines, 1724-1725. [NRS.RS18.10.1/3/4/24/81]

ROWAN, DAVID, in West Reston, sasines, 1675-1681. [NRS.RS18.3.330, etc]

ROWAT, JAMES, minister at Jedburgh, from 1732 until his death 23 June 1733. [F.2.127]

RULE, ANN, born 1690, died 29 October 1712. [Mindrum MI]

RULE, JOHN, born 1727, schoolmaster at Cranshaws for 48 years, died 21 September 1801, his spouse Janet Waite, born 1735, died 23 November 1818. [Cranshaws MI, Berwickshire]

RULE, ROBERT, of Peelwells, testament, 1691. C.L. [NRS]

RULE, THOMAS, a sergeant in the service of the East India Company, son of William Rule a maltster in Mordington, a sasine, 1755. [NRS.RS18.13.465]

RULE, WILLIAM, a bailie and maltster in Mordington, sasines, 1755-1766. [NRS.RS18.13.465; 15.218]

RUMNEY, JOSEPH, vicar of Berwick, a sasine, 1772. [NRS.RS18.16.160]

RUNCIEMAN, ALEXANDER, in Naburn, testament, 1671. C.L. [NRS]

RUNCIEMAN, JAMES, in Graden, testament, 1679. C.L. [NRS]

RUNCIEMAN, JAMES, a shoemaker in Cornhill, later a feuar in Coldstream, sasines, 1750-1754. [NRS.RS18.13.72/305/396]

RUSSELL, ALEXANDER, from Teviotdale, a member of the Scots Charitable Society of Boston, 1749. [NEHGS]

RUTHERFORD, ANDREW, born 1629, minister at Eccles in 1655, master of Jedburgh Grammar School 1660s. [F.2.13]

RUTHERFORD, ANNE, daughter of James Rutherford of Bowland and his wife Isabella Simpson, settled in Wilmington, North Carolina, married R. Shaw, died in Wilmington on 11 January 1767. [SM.29.166][RTI.Ped.]

The People of the Scottish Borders, 1650-1800

RUTHERFORD, BARBARA, daughter of James Rutherford of Bowland and his wife Isabella Simpson, settled in Wilmington, North Carolina, married Alexander Chapman, died in Wilmington in November 1763. [SM.26.55][RTI.Ped.]

RUTHERFORD, CICELY, daughter of John Rutherford provost of Jedburgh, a marriage contract, 1760. [NRS.CC18.7.249]

RUTHERFORD, DAVID, of Capehope, an advocate, a deed, 1761. [NRS.CC18.7.369]

RUTHERFORD, GEORGE, from Jedburgh, a surgeon's mate aboard the St Andrew bound from Leith to Darien 14 July 1698, testament, 1709, C.E. [NRS]

RUTHERFORD, GEORGE, a merchant in Glasgow, heir to his father Dr Thomas Rutherford of Sameesten, a physician in Jedburgh, 1799. [NRS.S/H]

RUTHERFORD, JAMES, son and heir of Robert Rutherford a surgeon apothecary in Jedburgh, 1710. [NRS.S/H]

RUTHERFORD, JOHN, born 1641, son of John Ruherford tacksman of Grundisnock and his wife Isabella Ker, master of Selkirk Grammar School from 1680, minister at Yarrow from 1691 until his death on 8 May 1710; husband of Christian [Shaw?], parents of Robert, John, and Jean. [F.2.197]

RUTHERFORD, JOHN, of Bowland, settled in Wilmington, North Carolina, before 1752. [NRS.RD3.171.273]

RUTHERFORD, JOHN, late of Bowland, son and heir of James Rutherford of Bowland, in the lands and barony of Stuartsfield, Jedburgh, 1753. [NRS.S/H]

RUTHERFORD, JOHN, of Edgertoun, a deed of factory, 1760. [NRS.CC18.7.287]

RUTHERFORD, JOHN, of Knowsouth, deeds, contracts, bonds, 1756-1761. [NRS.CC18.7.47/87/186/190/229/244/246/301/302/382]

RUTHERFORD, JOHN, portioner of Darnick, son and heir to his parents John Rutherford, portioner of Darnick, and Margaret Dalgleish, daughter of John Dalgleish, 1795. [NRS.S/H]

The People of the Scottish Borders, 1650-1800

RUTHERFORD, JOHN, of Knowsouth, heir and grandson of John Rutherford of Knowsouth, 1798. [NRS.S/H]

RUTHERFORD, JOHN, of Edgerston, heir to Richard Rutherford, master and commander in the Royal Navy, who died 7 December 1795, eldest son of the deceased Thomas Rutherford a physician in Barbados, 1804. [NRS.S/H]

RUTHERFORD, ROBERT, of Fairnalee, a deed, 1759. [NRS.CC18.7.221]

RUTHERFORD, ROBERT, of Knowsouth, deeds, 1761. [NRS.CC18.7.307/321/336/339]

RUTHERFORD, SIMEON, in Pitelsheugh, testament, 1687. C.L. [NRS]

RUTHERFORD, THOMAS, carrier in Langtoun, a deed, 1757. [NRS.CC18.7.61]

RUTHERFORD, THOMAS, son of William Rutherford deacon of the wrights in Jedburgh, a marriage contract, 1760. [NRS.CC18.7.249]

RUTHERFORD, Dr THOMAS, in Jedburgh, a deed, 1768; a sasine, 1769. [NRS.RD4.217.316; RS18.15.410]

RUTHERFORD, THOMAS, in Newton of Coldstream, a sasine, 1772. [NRS.RS18.16.197]

RUTHERFORD, THOMAS, eldest son of Andrew Rutherford a merchant in Jedburgh, died in Christiansted, St Croix, Danish West Indies, 22 November 1808. [SM.71.398][EA.4750]

RUTHERFORD, WALTER, born 29 December 1723 in Edgerston, Roxburghshire, son of Sir John Rutherford and his wife Elizabeth Cairncross, emigrated before 1758, a soldier and a merchant, settled in Hunterdon County, New York, died 10 January 1808 in New York. [NRS.RD2.210.911]

RUTHERFORD, WILLIAM, from Teviotdale, a member of the Scots Charitable Society of Boston, 1748. [NEHGS]

RUTHERFORD, WILLIAM, a shopkeeper in Kelso, 1785. [NRS.E326.4.1]

RUTHERFORD, WILLIAM, a shoemaker in Kelso, heir to his father George Rutherford in Kelso, 1790. [NRS.S/H]

The People of the Scottish Borders, 1650-1800

SADDLER, JAMES, a feuar in Duns, testament, 1735. C.L. [NRS]

SADDLER, JOHN, a maltman in Duns, sasines, 1703-1724. [NRS.RS18.6.455; 9.611]

SADDLER, ROBERT, a merchant in Duns, sasines, 1702-1722, [NRS.RS18.6.355; 9.527]; testament, 1726. C.L. [NRS]

SADDLER, WILLIAM, a maltman and feuar in Duns, testament, 1726. C.L. [NRS]

SAMSON, ROBERT, a mealmaker in Grueldykes, testament, 1713. C.L. [NRS]

SAMSON, JAMES, a wright in Duns, sasines, 1704-1734. [NRS.RS18.6.565; 10.513; 11.132]

SANDERSON, ADAM, precentor formerly schoolmaster in Eccles, sasines, 1706-1728. [NRS.RS18.7.127, etc]

SANDERSON, DAVID, born 1706, died 18 September 1772, his spouse Cisel Watson born 1690, died 27 December 1756. [Ayton MI, Berwickshire]; a sasine, 1762. [NRS.RS18.14.415]

SANDERSON, JAMES, a merchant in Hawick, a deed, 1761. [NRS.CC18.7.382]

SANDERSON, JAMES, born 1730, died 22 August 1800. [Ayton MI]

SANDERSON, JOHN, in Auchencraw, testament, 1715. C.L. [NRS]

SANDERSON, JOHN, a kilman in Home, testament, 1734. C.L. [NRS]

SANDERSON, JOHN, a baker in Duns, sasines, 1777-1778. [NRS.RS18.17.122/237]

SANDERSON, ROBERT, of Whiterig, a writer in Duns, a sasine, 1775, [NRS.RS18.16.414]; testament, 1777. C.L. [NRS]

SANDERSON, THOMAS, son of Charles Sanderson, a shoemaker in Earlston, sasines, 1747-1756. [NRS.RS18.12.339/340/493]

SANDERSON, WILLIAM, born 1667, tenant in Makerstoun New Mains, died 26 June 1744. [Mertoun MI, Berwickshire]

SANDILANDS, JOHN, of Middlethird, sasines, 1683. [NRS.RS18.4.374]

The People of the Scottish Borders, 1650-1800

SANSON, GEORGE, in Newbigging, testament, 1740. C.L. [NRS]

SANSON, JAMES, a mealmaker in Stabiwood, a sasine, 1758. [NRS.RS18.13.551]

SAWER, AGNES, in Coldstream, a sasine, 1664. [NRS.RS18.1.176]

SCOTT, ADAM, in Edgerton, a deed, 1758. [NRS.CC18.7.137]

SCOTT, ADAM, in Wauchope, a deed, 1757. [NRS.CC18.7.71]

SCOTT, ADAM, an innkeeper in Jedburgh, a deed, 1758. [NRS.CC18.7.138]

SCOTT, ADAM, a mason in Hawick, deeds, 1760. [NRS.CC18.7.291/298]

SCOTT, AGNES, in Wauchope, a deed, 1757. [NRS.CC18.7.71]

SCOTT, ALEXANDER, a flesher in Selkirk, a deed, 1756. [NRS.CC18.7.22]

SCOTT, ANDREW, a Covenanter from Teviotdale, was transported from Leith to Jamaica in July 1685, landed at Port Royal, Jamaica in November 1685. [RPCS.II.329][LJ.195]

SCOTT, ANDREW, in Selkirk, 1783. [NRS.E326.1.210]

SCOTT, CHARLES, of Cramshaugh, a deed, 1756. [NRS.CC18.7.22]

SCOTT, CHARLES, of Howcleugh, heir to his brother Walter Scott of Waughope, 1796.[NRS.S/H]

SCOTT, DAVID, in Thorniehall, a deed, 1757. [NRS.CC18.7.70]

SCOTT, FRANCIS, born 1749, in Damhead of Traquair, died 21 June 1806. [Longnewton MI, Roxburghshire]

SCOTT, GEORGE, in Mains, a deed, 1757. [NRS.CC18.7.116]

SCOTT, GEORGE, at Waterside, a deed, 1758. [NRS.CC18.7.145]

SCOTT, GEORGE, a merchant in Hawick, a marriage contract etc, 1761. [NRS.CC18.7.322/333]

SCOTT, GEORGE, a gardener in Kelso, Roxburghshire, 1784. [NRS.CS228.A.5.27.1]

The People of the Scottish Borders, 1650-1800

SCOTT, GIDEON, in Priesthaugh, deeds, 1758-1760. [NRS.CC18.7.168/278]

SCOTT, HENRY, portioner of Paxton, sasines, 1761-1777. [NRS.RS18.14.356; 17.171]

SCOTT, HUGH, minister at Oxnam, at Galashiels 1672-1688, at Stow, 1688-. [F.2.177]

SCOTT, HUGH, son of Hugh Scott of Galashiels, Selkirkshire, died 1699 at Darien, testament 1708. [NRS.CC8.8.84]

SCOTT, HUGH, of Gala, son and heir to his father John Scott who died 17 March 1785, 1794. [NRS.S/H]

SCOTT, JAMES, minister at Galashiels 1689-1690, died in Edinburgh, 17 June 1715. [F.2.177]

SCOTT, JAMES, of Bowhill, a sasine, 1688. [NRS.RS18.5.39]

SCOTT, JAMES, born 1701, tenant in Denholm, died 28 April 1782, his spouse Jean Kerswell, born 1703, died 22 December 1779. [Cavers MI]

SCOTT, JAMES, in Dimpleknow, a deed, 1757. [NRS.CC18.7.115]

SCOTT, JAMES, in Hermiston, a deed, 1758. [NRS.CC18.7.147]

SCOTT, JAMES, a baxter in Hawick, a deed, 1757. [NRS.CC18.7.124]

SCOTT, JAMES, a carrier in Hawick, deeds, 1758-1760. [NRS.CC18.7.124/136/172/295]

SCOTT, JAMES, tenant in Hoperig, testament, 1768. C.L. [NRS]

SCOTT, JAMES, tenant in Newhall, died 8 October 1789. [Longnewton MI, Roxburghshire]

SCOTT, JAMES, born 1713, in Kirkton parish, died 12 February 1795; his spouse Janet Fletcher, born 1726, died 6 September 1794. [Cavers MI]

SCOTT, JANET, in Wauchope, a deed, 1757. [NRS.CC18.7.71]

SCOTT, JEAN, born 1741, spouse to James Hapkirk tenant of Whithope Mill, died 11 June 1817. [Cavers MI]

The People of the Scottish Borders, 1650-1800

SCOTT, JOHN, minister at Hawick from 1657 to 1662, husband of (1) Marion Livingston, (2) Elizabeth Anderson. [F.2.113]

SCOTT, JOHN, son of James Scott of Thirleston, Berwickshire, died at Darien, testament, 1707. [NRS.CC8.8.83]

SCOTT, JOHN, born 1660, tenant in Denholm, died 1738, his son William Scott, born 1704, died 1749. [Cavers MI]

SCOTT, JOHN, of Ashtrees, deeds, 1757-1760. [NRS.CC18.7.96/204/205/287]

SCOTT, JOHN, of Belford, a deed, 1761. [NRS.CC18.7.362]

SCOTT, JOHN, a dyster in Jedburgh, a deed, 1756. [NRS.CC18.7.43]

SCOTT, JOHN, a merchant in Hawick, a deed, 1758. [NRS.CC18.7.142]

SCOTT, JOHN, a shoemaker in Jedburgh, a deed, 1758. [NRS.CC18.7.177]

SCOTT, JOHN, in Deanbrae, a deed, 1759. [NRS.CC18.7.199]

SCOTT, JOHN, of Gorrenberry, a deed, 1759. [NRS.CC18.7.230]

SCOTT, JOHN, of Lees, a deed, 1760. [NRS.CC18.7.225]

SCOTT, JOHN, in Wholehope, a deed, 1761. [NRS.CC18.7.225]

SCOTT, JOHN, a carrier in Hawick, a deed, 1761. [NRS.CC18.7.345]

SCOTT, MARGARET, spouse to Walter Riddel miller at Martin Miln, testament, 1728. C.L. [NRS]

SCOTT, Sir PATRICK, of Ancrum, sasines, 1693-1701. [NRS.RS18.5.224; 6.187]

SCOTT, PATRICK, in Borthaugh, deeds, 1757-1762. [NRS.CC18.7.110/385]

SCOTT, PATRICK, in Whitelaw, a deed, 1760. [NRS.CC18.7.243]

SCOTT, RICHARD, born 1641, third son of George Scott of Sinton and his wife Mary Gladstanes of Dod, educated at Edinburgh University 1658, minister at Ashkirk, Selkirkshire, from 1685 until 1689, died 25 May 1722. [F.2.169]

SCOTT, RICHARD, minister at Cranshaws from 1759 until 1761. [F.2.6]

The People of the Scottish Borders, 1650-1800

SCOTT, ROBERT, baptised in Duns, Berwickshire, 1708, to Madeira as a merchant during 1720s, moved to London around 1736; by 1739 he was a merchant in Madeira, possibly linked to the Scotts of Harden. [NRS.GD157.2267]; 1749, Robert Scott, merchant in Madeira and London, deed of factory, [NRS.RD4.176/1.155];he was trading with South Carolina in 1756. [NRS.GD219/290] [NA.CO137.17] [CSPCol.XLIII, 1737] [Livros dos Saidas # 252, fos. 53/69, Arquivo Nacional da Torre do Tombo, Lisbon]

SCOTT, ROBERT, born 1708, a husbandman from Berwick, emigrated via London to Maryland on 7 January 1736. [CLRO/AIA]

SCOTT, ROBERT, of Burnhead, a deed, 1755. [NRS.CC18.7.1]

SCOTT, ROBERT, a bailie of Hawick, a deed, 1758. [NRS.CC18.7.150]

SCOTT, ROBERT, of Trabroun, a merchant in London, and his son Robert Scott, sasines, 1771-1776. [NRS.RS18.16.127/280/; 17.88/91]

SCOTT, ROBERT, an innkeeper in Hawick, a deed, 1762. [NRS.CC18.7.382]

SCOTT, ROBERT, in Selkirk, 1783. [NRS.E326.1.210]

SCOTT, THOMAS, from Selkirk, emigrated via London to Pennsylvania in February 1721. [CLRO/AIA]

SCOTT, THOMAS, in Clarilaw, a deed, 1760. [NAS.CC18.7.241]

SCOTT, THOMAS, of Stonedge, a contract and tack, 1757-1758. [NRS.CC18.7.320]

SCOTT, THOMAS, a merchant in Kirkhope, a deed, 1761. [NRS.CC18.7.320]

SCOTT, WALTER, of Raeburn, third son of Walter Scott of Harden, a Quaker 1665. [RPCS.3/II.57]

SCOTT, WALTER, of Hurdlaw, a merchant in Kelso, a sasine, 1704. [NRS.RS18.6.554]

SCOTT, WALTER, in Lymecleugh, heir to his grand-uncle Andrew Turnbull, writer in Hawick, 1706. [SHR.14]

SCOTT, WALTER, minister at Westruther, testament, 1738. C.L. [NRS]

The People of the Scottish Borders, 1650-1800

SCOTT, WALTER, of Howcleugh, a deed, 1758. [NRS.CC18.7.168]

SCOTT, WALTER, of Crumhaugh, a bond, 1758. [NRS.CC18.7.144]

SCOTT, WALTER, in Wauchope, a deed, 1757. [NRS.CC18.7.71]

SCOTT, WALTER, a carrier in Hawick, a deed, 1761. [NRS.CC18.7.377]

SCOTT, Sir WILLIAM, of Harden, testaments, 1708/1715/1728. C.L. [NRS]

SCOTT, Sir WILLIAM, of Ancrum, a contract and bond, 1757-1761. [NRS.CC18.7.87/339]

SCOTT, WILLIAM, of Burnhead, a deed of attorney, 1757. [NRS.CC18.7.121]

SCOTT, WILLIAM, in Hawick, deeds, 1759-1760. [NRS.CC18.7.227/299]

SCOTT, WILLIAM, in Tundside, a deed, 1759. [NRS.CC18.7.204]

SCOTT, WILLIAM, in Trends, a deed, 1757. [NRS.CC18.7.87]

SCOTT, WILLIAM, a carrier in Langton, a deed, 1757. [NRS.CC18.7.109]

SCOTT, WILLIAM, a mason in Caltersheugh, deeds, 1758. [NRS.CC18.7.149/150]

SCOTT, WILLIAM, a shoemaker in Hawick, a deed, 1757. [NRS.CC18.7.117]

SCOTT, WILLIAM, a gardener in Kelso, Roxburghshire, 1784. [NRS.CS228.A.5.27.1]

SCOTT and FRASER, in Gothenburg, Sweden, a sasine, 1777. [NRS.RS18.17.139]

SCOUGALL, Sir JAMES, of Whythill, a sasine, 1702. [NRS.RS18.6.390]

SCOUGALL, JOHN, in New Mains of Mordington, testament, 1788. C.L. [NRS]

SCOUGALL, THOMAS, in Birkensyde, sasines, 1688-1701. [NRS.RS18.5.62; 6.229]

SCOUGALL, WILLIAM, in Cranshaw Milne, testament, 1688. C.L. [NRS]

SCOULLAR, DANIEL, a skinner in Duns, sasines, 1677-1678. [NRS.RS18.4.59/90]

The People of the Scottish Borders, 1650-1800

SCOULLAR, GEORGE, in Hutton, a sasine, 1661, [NRS.RS18.4.162]; testament, 1665. C.L. [NRS]

SCOULLAR, RALPH, portioner in Hutton, testament, 1665. C.L. [NRS]

SCOULLAR, RODOLPH, in Hutton, a sasine, 1670. [NRS.RS18.2.266]

SEATON, JOHN, son of James Seaton in Chapel Lauder, Berwickshire, a minister aboard the Caledonia from Leith to Darien on 14 July 1698, testament, 1707, C.E. [NRS.CC8.8.83]

SEATON, MARGARET, relict of William Robertson a merchant in Eyemouth, testaments, 1730/1732/1746. C.L. [NRS]

SEATON, WILLIAM, son of Alexander Seaton of Kilriach, sasines, 1687-1693. [NRS.RS18.5.4/235/237]

SEDGELEY, ROBERT, a slater in Duns, husband of Margaret Landels born 1768, died 16 February 1800. [Duns MI, Berwickshire]

SELBY, EPHRAIM, a merchant in Duns, and his brother Robertt Selby, a sasine, 1772. [NRS.RS18.16.166]

SEMPILL, JOHN, in Uxtoun, parish of Ginglekirk, testament, 1663. C.L. [NRS]

SEMPLE, GABRIEL, born 1632, son of Bryce Semple of Cathcart, minister at Jedburgh from 1690 until his death 8 August 1706, husband of (1) Margaret Murray, (2) Alison Riddell, (3) Margaret Carr. [F.2.127]

SEMPLE, ROBERT, of Fulwood, sasines, 1695-1719. [NRS.RS18.5.283; 8.449/471/583; 9.299]

SHARP, HENRY, in Longformacus, a sasine, 1778. [NRS.RS18.17.242]

SHARP, KATHARINE, spouse to John Cochrane, testament, 1670. C.L. [NRS]

SHARP, THOMAS, minister at Hawick 1784-1789. [F.2.115]

SHAW, HENRY, minister at Cockburnspath, and his son John Shaw, a sasine, 1708. [NRS.RS18.7.487]

SHAW, ROBERT, a weaver in Puddingraw, a sasine, 1770. [NRS.RS18.15.434]

The People of the Scottish Borders, 1650-1800

SHEREST, EDWARD, in East Nisbet, testament, 1689. C.L. [NRS]

SHERIFF, GEORGE, died 1 March 1771, his wife Christian Adamson died 1 June 1786, Alexander Sheriff died 4 July 1797. [Abbey St Bathans MI, Berwickshire]

SHERIFF, JOHN, son of Patrick Sheriff in Heloun, a sasine, 1692. [NRS.RS18.5.178]

SHERIFF, PATRICK, a baxter in Duns, testament, 1715. C.L.[NRS]

SHERIFFLAW, DAVID, a cooper in Eyemouth, a sasine, 1770. [NRS.RS18.15.423]

SHERIFFLAW, GEORGE, a shoemaker in Eyemouth, sasines, 1756-1769. [NRS.RS18.13.501; 15.398]

SHERILAW, WALTER, a shoemaker in Eyemouth, testament, 1781. C.L. [NRS]

SHIELDS, ALEXANDER, born 1661, a minister from Berwickshire, a refugee in the Netherlands from 1680-1690. [SEC][REPE]

SHIELDS, ANDREW, a baxter in Earlston, sasines, 1743-1750. [NRS.RS18.12.33; 13.15]

SHIELD, WILLIAM, a messenger in Earlston, a sasine, 1750. [NRS.RS18.13.15]

SHIELL, ARCHIBALD, in Cocklaw, Channelkirk, testament, 1673. C.L. [NRS]

SHIELL, JAMES, in Holehead, a deed, 1758. [NRS.CC18.7.130]

SHIELL, THOMAS, in Hieton Miln, a deed, 1759. [NRS.CC18.7.224]

SHIELL, THOMAS, tenant in Elsinure, testament, 1772. C.L. [NRS]

SHILLINGLAW, JOHN, in Thirlston Mill, testament, 1683. C.L. [NRS]

SHIREFF, WILLIAM, born 1701, died 14 December 1736. [Abbey St Bathans MI, Berwickshire]

SHIREFF, WILLIAM, born 1735, died 4 December 1817. [Abbey St Bathans, MI, Berwickshire]

SHORT, ARCHIBALD, in Fimelhaugh, testament, 1732. C.L. [NRS]

SHORT, THOMAS, a shoemaker in Duns, sasines, 1758. [NRS.RS18.13.540/542]

The People of the Scottish Borders, 1650-1800

SHORT, THOMAS, in Thimble Hall, Duns, testament, 1764. C.L. [NRS]

SHORTREAD, JAMES, of Easter Essenside, a deed, 1760. [NRS.CC18.7.247]

SIBBALD, HENRY, a farmer in Renton, a sasine, 1718. [NRS.RS18.9.198]

SIBBALD, MATTHEW, in Horndean, sasines, 1765-1770. [NRS.RS18.15.147/448]

SIBBETT, ISOBEL, spouse of John Home in Stand-the-Lane, testament, 1672. C.L. [NRS]

SIMPSON, ALEXANDER, a gardener in Dryburgh, sasines, 1744-1750. [NRS.RS18.12.131/135/243; 13.9; 15.278]

SIMPSON, CHRISTIAN, spouse to James Law in West Nisbet, testament, 1671. C.L. [NRS]

SIMPSON, GEORGE, portioner of Huntlywood, a sasine, 1779. [NRS.RS18.17.386]

SIMPSON, JOHN, from Gariside, Roxburghshire, a Covenanter who was transported from Leith to Jamaica in August 1685, landed at Port Royal in November 1685. [RPCS.II.330][Edinburgh Tolbooth Register.369][LJ.15]

SIMPSON, JOHN, of Grueldykes, a merchant in Sunbury, Georgia, 1774. [NRS.CS16.1.157/165]

SIMPSON, JOHN, in Eyemouth, testament, 1775. C.L. [NRS]

SIMPSON, MARY, relict of John Gardener a gardener in Hawick, a marriage contract, 1761. [NRS.CC18.7.322]

SIMPSON, PATRICK, in Redpath, a sasine, 1767. [NRS.RS18.15.278]

SIMPSON, SAMUEL, of Flemington, a merchant in Berwick, sasines, 1758-1763. [NRS.RS18.13.538; 14.477]

SIMPSON, THOMAS, M.D., in Duns, testament, 1753. C.L. [NRS]

SIMPSON, WILLIAM, a smith in Coldingham, a sasine, 1678. [NRS.RS18.4.103]

SINCLAIR, DANIEL, minister at Longformacus, testaments, 1735/1742. C.L. [NRS]

The People of the Scottish Borders, 1650-1800

SINCLAIR, GEORGE, a wright in Birgham, testament, 1751. C.L. [NRS]

SINCLAIR, Sir HENRY, of Longformacus, a sasine, 1769. [NRS.RS18.15.380]

SINCLAIR, JOHN, a merchant in Eyemouth, sasines, 1691-1692. [NRS.RS18.5.173/174/185/331]

SINCLAIR, Sir ROBERT, of Longformacus, testament, 1732. C.L. [NRS]

SINCLAIR, WILLIAM, in Home, testament, 1740. C.L. [NRS]

SINCLAIR, WILLIAM, a shoemaker in Eyemouth, a sasine, 1675. [NRS.RS18.3.317]

SKAILLES, JAMES, son of John Skailles, a weaver in Duns, sasines, 1673. [NRS.RS18.3.103/104]

SKAILLES, NICOLAS, in Chirnside, testament, 1680. C.L. [NRS]

SKED, JOHN, born 1741, minister at Abbey St Bathans from 1774-1813, died 23 January 1818, his wife Margaret Renton, born 1766, died 19 February 1796, parents of Margaret and William. [Abbey St Bathans MI, Berwickshire][F.2.3]

SKED, WILLIAM, in Fawside, testament, 1683. C.L. [NRS]

SKED, WILLIAM, a baxter in Home, sasines, 1748-1751. [NRS.RS18.12.428; 13.156]

SKIERLAW, DAVID, a cooper in Eyemouth, testament, 1792. C.L. [NRS]

SKLAITHER, ANDREW, a weaver in Adinstoun, testament, 1663. C.L. [NRS]

SLEIGH, ADAM, tenant in Rules Mains, testament, 1774. C.L. [NRS]

SLEIGH, JOHN, a feuar in Duns, formerly a herd in Blackhouse, sasines, 1752-1755. [NRS.RS18.13.258/402/444]

SLEIGH, PATRICK, tenant in Preston, a sasine, 1759, [NRS.RS18.14.22]; testament, 1773. C.L. [NRS]

SLOWAN, ALEXANDER, a slater in Kelso, heir to his father Andrew Slowan, a slater there, 1725. [NRS.S/H]

The People of the Scottish Borders, 1650-1800

SMAILL, ADAM, a shoemaker in Jedburgh, a deed, 1758. [NRS.CC18.7.173]

SMAIL, HENRY, schoolmaster in Longnewton, died March 1741. [Longnewton MI. Roxburghshire]

SMAILL, WILLIAM, a tailor in Ancrum, heir to his uncle George Smaill in Ancrum, 1794. [NRS.S/H]

SMALL, ADAM, born 1746, late tenant in Belches Mill, died 7 May 1806. [Longnewton MI, Roxburghshire]

SMALL, ALEXANDER, a mason in Kelso, a sasine, 1683. [NRS.RS18.3.353]

SMALL, JOHN, in Hobton, testament, 1671. C.L. [NRS]

SMEWREY, CORNELIUS, born 1662, a weaver from Berwick, emigrated via London to Barbados on 15 May 1686. [CLRO/AIA]

SMITH, ALEXANDER, a weaver in Lambden, a sasine, 1743. [NRS.RS18.12.3]

SMITH, ALEXANDER, tenant of Birgham, testament, 1786. C.L. [NRS]

SMITH, ANDREW, born 1708, tenant in Longnewton, died 15 January 1781, his spouse Helen Balmer born 1714, died 16 November 1774. [Longnewton MI, Roxburghshire]

SMITH, ARCHIBALD, of Evelaw, tenant in Colelaw, sasines, 1747-1754, [NRS.RS18.12.361; 13.402]; testament, 1755. C.L. [NRS]

SMITH, GEORGE, quartermaster in Captain Blair's troop of the Royal British Dragoons, a sasine, 1756. [NRS.RS18.13.492]

SMITH, JAMES, tenant in Longnewton, spouse of E.... Clerk born 1696, died 14 September 1734. [Longnewton MI, Roxburghshire]

SMITH, JAMES, in Peebles, a bond, 1757. [NRS.RD4.218.504]

SMITH, JAMES, a wright in Ayton, a sasine, 1772. [NRS.RS18.16.177]

SMITH, JOHN, a wright and portioner in Darnick, heir to his father Andrew Smith a portioner there, 1790. [NRS.S/H]

SMITH, MARK, of Quixwood, a sasine, 1774. [NRS.RS18.16.329]

The People of the Scottish Borders, 1650-1800

SMITH, Mrs MARY, born 1759, wife of Adam Smith, died at Horseridge on 1 October 1798. [Mindrum MI]

SMITH, PATRICK, of Hillend, testament, 1756. C.L. [NRS]

SMITH, RICHARD, a schoolmaster in Coldingham, a sasine, 1716. [NRS.RS18.9.130]

SMITH, WILLIAM, bailie of Lauder, testament, 1722. C.L. [NRS]

SMITH, WILLIAM, tenant in Denholm, husband of Helen Douglas born 1694, died 18 March 1736, parents of George Smith, born 1723, died 25 July 1727. [Cavers MI]

SMITH, WILLIAM, born 1736, died 27 May 1829, his wife Elisabeth Martin, born 1770, died 7 June 1835, a son John Smith, born 1807, died in Tarbolton, Ontario, 24 November 1879. [Duns MI, Berwickshire]

SMITTON, WILLIAM, born 1701, a weaver in West Mains of Buncle, died 4 January 1767. [Abbey St Bathans MI, Berwickshire]

SOMERVELL, GEORGE, tenant in Headshaw, testament, 1686. C,L, [NRS]

SOMERVELL, JOHN, tenant in Braefoot, Channelkirk, testament, 1719. C.L. [NRS]

SOMERVILLE, ALEXANDER, born 1772 in Roxburghshire, son of Dr Archibald Somerville, a book-seller in New York by 1798, died in New Orleans on 4 September 1804. [St Andrew's Society of NY.II.342]

SOMERVILLE, GEORGE, of Airhouse, formerly in Cathrae, sasines, 1714. [NRS.RS18.8.548/550]

SOMERVILLE, JOHN, a merchant in Coldstream, a sasine, 1702. [NRS.RS18.6.305]

SOMERVILLE, THOMAS, born 15 February 1741, son of Rev. William Somerville in Hawick, minister at Jedburgh from 1773 until his death on 16 May 1830, husband of Martha Charters, parents of William, Christian, Samuel, Janet, Janet, Martha, and James. [F.2.128]

The People of the Scottish Borders, 1650-1800

SOMERVILLE, WILLIAM, born 1691, son of Thomas Somerville minister at Cavers, minister at Hawick from 1732 until his death on 8 February 1757, husband of (1) Janet Grierson, (2) Isabel Scott. [F.2.115]

SPARK, WILLIAM, born 1713, died 4 November 1795. [Ayton MI]

SPAVIN, JOHN, a weaver in Coldingham, a sasine, 1722. [NAS.RS18.9.498]

SPEED, ROBERT, in Slighhouses, sasines, 1702-1708. [NRS.RS18.6.365; 7.403]

SPEED, WILLIAM, minister at Botraphennie, residing in Netherbyres, Ayton, testament, 1706. C.L. [NRS]

SPEEDING, THOMAS, in Harlaw, testament, 1733. C.L. [NRS]

SPEEDIN, THOMAS, portioner in Bowden, son and heir to William Speedin a portioner there, 1793. [NRS.S/H]

SPEIRS, ADAM, a tailor in Woolstruther, a sasine, 1776. [NRS.RS18.17.36]

SPEIRS, JAMES, a herd in Idington Mains, Chirnside, testament, 1686. C.L. [NRS]

SPEIRS, JAMES, son of James Speirs, a seaman in Eyemouth, a sasine 1756. [NRS.RS18.13.502]

SPEIRS, JOHN, tenant in Whiteburn, testament, 1776. C.L. [NRS]

SPEIRS, WILLIAM, a wright in Coldstream, a sasine, 1768. [NRS.RS18.15.324]

SPENCE, ALEXANDER, a merchant in Duns, Berwickshire, a bankrupt who absconded to America around 1796. [NRS.CS230.Seqn.2/3]

SPENCE, JOHN, in Duns, testament, 1674. C.L. [NRS]

SPENCE, JOHN, a skinner and feuar in Duns, husband of Margaret Scott born 1746, died 2 March 1783. [Duns MI, Berwickshire]

SPENCE, ROBERT, servant to George Aitchison in New Mills, a sasine, 1772. [NRS.RS18.16.159]

SPENCE, ROBERT, late of Jamaica now in Newcastle, son and heir of Helen Spence in Kelso widow of Robert Spence there, 1796. [NRS.S/H]

The People of the Scottish Borders, 1650-1800

SPIDIN, Mrs JANE, born 1736, wife of William Spidin in Bowden, died in Kentucky 1819. [Longnewton MI, Roxburghshire]

SPOTSWOOD, ALEXANDER, of Crumstaine, an advocate, sasines, 1670-1674, [NRS.RS18.2.261/353, etc]; testaments 1676/1677. C.L. [NRS]

SPOTSWOOD, JAMES, a tailor and feuar in Kelso, residing in Home, testament, 1747. C.L. [NRS]

SPOTTISWOODE, JOHN, of Spottiswoode, died 11 March 1793, his wife Mary Thomson, died 10 May 1784. [Westruther MI, Berwickshire]

SPOUSE, WILLIAM, a butcher in Coldingham, sasines, 1748-1753. [NRS.RS18.12.446/473; 13.202/303]

SPOUSE, WILLIAM, a baker in Coldingham, testament, 1791. C.L. [NRS]

SPROTT, WILLIAM, of Clerklees, sasines, 1769-1772. [NRS.RS18.15.388/424; 16.48/190]

STARK, DAVID, minister at Stitchill, his widow Elizabeth Courtney, their sons David and Robert Stark, a sasine, 1688. [NRS.RS18.5.41]

STAVERT, THOMAS, born 1709, tenant in Colliforthill, died 16 June 1794. [Cavers MI]

STEEL, DAVID, a smith in Ramrigg and portioner of Hornden, a sasine, 1750. [NRS.RS18.13.35]

STEEL, HENRY, a merchant in Duns, sasines, 1772-1774. [NRS.RS18.16.179/210/313/358]

STEEL, JAMES, a tailor in Woolstruther, a sasine, 1776. [NRS.RS18.17.27]

STEEL, ROBERT, son of Robert Steel, a weaver in Coldstream, a sasine, 1762. [NRS.RS18.14.390]

STEELL, THOMAS, a weaver in Hutton, testament, 1798. C.L. [NRS]

STENHOUSE, ALEXANDER, servant to the Earl of Home, a sasine, 1720. [NRS.RS18.9.403]

The People of the Scottish Borders, 1650-1800

STENHOUSE, ANDREW, born 1681, tenant in Newton, died March 1758, his spouse Margaret Bowie, born 1683, died April 1763. [Nenthorn MI]

STENHOUSE, ARCHIBALD, in Oldtown of Coldstream, a sasine, 1710. [NRS.RS18.8.91]

STENHOUSE, THOMAS, in Coldstream, sasines, 1671. [NRS.RS18.1.215; 2.320]

STENHOUSE, WILLIAM, in Newton, testament, 1676. C.L. [NRS]

STENTOUN, SAMUEL, a merchant in Berwick, a sasine, 1721. [NRS.RS18.9.464]

STEPHEN, MATTHEW, in Coldingham, sasines, 1719. [NRS.RS18.9.309/316]

STEVENSON, GEORGE, in Tweedmill, the younger, a sasine, 1664. [NRS.RS18.1.247]

STEVENSON, GEORGE, in Hobkirk, deeds, 1758. [NRS.CC18.7.128/129]

STEVENSON, GEORGE, in Kirkstyle, a deed, 1759. [NRS.CC18.7.205]

STEVENSON, HAY, from the Borders, a merchant in New York from 1783, married Jessie Graham 29 July 1790, father of John Graham Stevenson, died 24 September 1799. [St Andrew's Society of NY.II.189]

STEVENSON, JOHN, of Plewland, testament, 1720. C.L. [NRS]

STEVENSON, JOHN, a cooper and merchant, sasines, 1766. [NRS.RS18.15.196/210]

STEVENSON, WILLIAM, a wright in Kennetsideheads, testament, 1716. C.L. [NRS]

STEVENSON, WILLIAM, in Birgham, sasines, 1720-1722. [NRS.RS18.9.383/502]

STEVENSON, WILLIAM, a mason in Birgham, testament, 1744. C.L. [NRS]

STEWART, CLARA, spouse to John Cumming minister at Eyemouth, testament, 1714. C.L. [NRS]

STEWART, Sir JOHN, of Allanbank, sasines, 1709-1716. [NRS.RS18.8.9/15; 9.108]

The People of the Scottish Borders, 1650-1800

STEWART, JOHN, a butcher in Kelso, a deed, 1758. [NRS.CC18.7.148]

STEWART, Sir ROBERT, of Allanbank, testaments, 1707/1729. C.L. [NRS]

STEWART, ROBERT, at Ashybank, a deed, 1760. [NRS.CC18.7.300]

STEWART, ROBERT, a wright in Lilliesleaf, a deed, 1756. [NRS.CC18.7.47]

STEWART, ROBERT, a butcher in Kelso, son and heir of Richard Stewart a butcher there, 1796. [NRS.S/H]

STEWART, THOMAS, a farmer in Kelso, Roxburghshire, versus Jean Gascoigne his spouse, daughter of Thomas Gascoigne, a shoemaker in Kelso, divorce, 1799. [NRS.CC8.6.1066]

STEWART, WALTER, of Barnhill, son of Baillie Matthew Stewart in Newton Mearns, educated at Edinburgh and Leyden Universities, minister at Ashkirk from 1730 until his death on 15 April 1762; husband of Mary Duncanson, parents of Mary, Matthew, Helen, Margaret, James, and Isabella. [F.2.169]

STIRLING, MABEL, from Roxburghshire, a gypsy who was transported from Glasgow to Virginia on 1 January 1715. [GR.530]

STIRLING, THOMAS, in Birkhillside, testament, 1782.C.L. [NRS]

STODDART, JOHN, of Camiestoun, sasines, 1700-1709. [NRS.RS18.6.161; 7.457/512]

STODDART, MARION, in Gordon Milne, testament, 1675. C.L. [NRS]

STORIE, ELIZABETH, relict of James Oswald schoolmaster of Coldstream, testament, 1682. C.L. [NRS]

STORIE, JOSEPH, in Hutton, formerly in Borwickhill, a sasine, 1779. [NRS.RS18.17.275]

STOW, BLAKE, a merchant in Berwick, a sasine, 1766. [NRS.RS18.15.211]

STOWARD, JOHN, a merchant in Berwick, sasines, 1773-1779. [NRS.RS18.16.215; 17.305]

STRACHAN, WILLIAM, in Duns, sasines, 1659-1691. [NRS.RS18.4.108, etc]

The People of the Scottish Borders, 1650-1800

STRAITH, ALEXANDER, in Hornden, testament, 1680. C.L. [NRS]

STRATON, JAMES, minister at Eyemouth, sasine, 1659. [NRS.RS18.4.40]

STRATON, PATRICK, in Fosterland, testament, 1653. C.L. [NRS]

STUART, Lady CHRISTIAN ELIZABETH, daughter of John Stuart of Traquair, Peebles-shire, and his wife Christian Anstruther, emigrated to Virginia before 1779, wife of Cyrus Griffen. [NRS.RD3.239.683]

SUDDANE, JANET, spouse to Charles Thomson a flesher in Lauder, testament, 1704. C.L. [NRS]

SUDDAN, JOHN, in Dryburgh, and his son Thomas Sudden, sasines, 1648-1673. [NRS.RS18.3.436, etc]

SWANSTON, CHARLES, in Northfield, Coldingham, testament, 1782. C.L. [NRS]

SWANSTON, DAVID, in Birgham, testament, 1748. C.L. [NRS]

SWANSTON, JOHN, a Customs officer at Coldingham, sasines, 1763-1765. [NRS.RS18.14.481; 15.101]

SWANSTON, JOHN, tenant in Floors, testament, 1788. C.L. [NRS]

SWANSTON, PATRICK, in Coldingham, a sasine, 1754. [NRS.RS18.13.354]

SWANSTON, WILLIAM, a brewer in Gunsgreen, testament, 1782. C.L. [NRS]

SWINTON, Sir ALEXANDER, of that Ilk, testament, 1653. C.L. [NRS]

SWINTON, Sir ALEXANDER, of Mersington, Eccles, testaments, 1707/1718. C.L. [NRS]

SWINTON, ARCHIBALD, of Manderston, sasines, 1779. [NRS.RS18.394/395]

SWINTON, Sir JOHN, of Swinton, a Quaker in prison, 1660s. [RPCS.3.III.130/155/615]

SWINTON, JOHN, minister at Cranshaws from 1674 until 1706, spouse of Katherine Gray. [F.2.6]

The People of the Scottish Borders, 1650-1800

SWINTON, JOHN, from Teviotdale, Roxburghshire, a Quaker who was transported from Leith aboard the Henry and Francis of Newcastle bound for East New Jersey on 5 September 1685. [RPCS.II.154]

SWINTON, JOHN, minister at Cranshaws, testament, 1714. C.L. [NRS]

SWYN, ARCHIBALD, a mason in Swinton, a sasine, 1778. [NRS.RS18.17.203]

SWYN, GEORGE, a glover at Duns, sasines, 1700-1708. [NRS.RS18.6.30; 7.475]

SYDSERFF, ARCHIBALD, of Ruchley, sasines, 1665-1666. [NRS.RS18.1.289/349]

SYMINGTON, DAVID, a boatbuilder in Eyemouth, a sasine, 1773. [NRS.RS18.16.221]

SYMINGTON, JOHN, born 1675, died 1755. [Ayton MI, Berwickshire]

SYMINGTON, WILLIAM, born 1642, indweller in Prenderguest, died 1725. [Ayton MI, Berwickshire]

TAIT, ALEXANDER, a gardener in Preston, sasines, 1747-1751. [NRS.RS18.12.376/378; 13.118/139]

TAIT, GEORGE, born 1600, died 4 October 1675. [Mindrum MI]

TAIT, GEORGE, a steward in Allback, thereafter in Kimmerghame, testament, 1738. C.L. [NRS]

TAIT, GEORGE, born 1701, from Yeavering, died 6 July 1756. [Mindrum MI]

TAIT, JAMES, son of James Tait in Auldhamstocks, a sasine, 1682. [NRS.RS18.4.284]

TAIT, JOHN, a tailor in Coldstream, a sasine, 1761. [NRS.RS18.14.376]

TAIT, JOSEPH, of Langrigg, a sasine, 1767. [NRS.RS18.15.251]

TAIT, ROBERT, a shoemaker in Coldstream, sasines, 1698. [NRS.RS18.5.404/405]

TAIT, THOMAS, in Nether Huntlie, testament, 1701. C.L. [NRS]

The People of the Scottish Borders, 1650-1800

TAIT, WALTER, an innkeeper in Melrose, deeds, 1756-1757. [NRS.CC18.7.48/103]

TAIT, WILLIAM, in Crawhill, a deed, 1760. [NRS.CC18.7.242]

TAIT, WILLIAM, an innkeeper in Melrose, a deed, 1759. [NRS.CC18.7.227]

TAYLOR, GAVIN, a shoemaker in Coldstream, a sasine, 1679. [NRS.RS18.4.137]

TAYLOR, JOHN, in Coldstream, sasines, 1768-1773. [NRS.RS18.15.326; 16.95/288]

TAYLOR, MARGARET, in Systerpath Milne, testament, 1671. C.L. [NRS]

TAYLOR, THOMAS, in Fala, a deed, 1775. [NRS.RD3.234.630]

TELFER, ALEXANDER, of Kimmerhame, sasines, 1762. [NRS.RS18.14.385/421]

TELFER, CHARLES, born 1693, son of Charles Telfer a bailie of Edinburgh, minister at Hawick 1728-1730, died July 1731, husband of Katherine Elliot a widow. [F.2.115]

TELFORD, JAMES, in Letham, a deed, 1758. [NRS.CC18.7.145]

TELFORD, JAMES, in Whitehomes, a deed, 1757. [NRS.CC18.7.96]

TEMPILL, GEORGE, in Foulden, testament, 1671. C.L. [NRS]

TEMPLE, JOHN, a shoemaker in Duns, his spouse Jean Angus, and sons George and Robert Temple, sasines, 1729, 1752. [NRS.RS18.10.314; 13.240]

TEMPLE, WILLIAM, from Linton, Roxburghshire, was transported from Leith aboard the <u>St Michael of Scarborough</u> bound for the West Indies on 12 December 1685. [RPCS.6.76]

TENNANT, JOHN, of Houndaxwood, and his daughters Margaret and Elizabeth spouse of James Cook schoolmaster of Bathgate, a sasine, 1719. [NRS.RS18.9.334]

THINN, LEONARD, in Blyth, testament, 1668. C.L. [NRS]

THOMSON, ADAM, tenant in Newton of Coldstream, testament, 1739. C.L. [NRS]

The People of the Scottish Borders, 1650-1800

THOMSON, ALEXANDER, a merchant in Lauder, sasines, 1728-1754. [NRS.RS18.10.310; 13.358]

THOMSON, ANDREW, in Glasgow, son and heir of James Thomson a mason in Denholm, 1794. [NRS.S/H]

THOMSON, GEORGE, an armourer in Duns, sasines, 1642-1658. [NRS.RS18.3.364; 4.23]

THOMSON, ISOBEL, relict of John Broun a merchant in Coldstream, testament, 1730. C.L. [NRS]

THOMSON, JAMES, a merchant in Kelso, a sasine, 1706. [NRS.RS18.7.118]

THOMSON, JAMES, a carrier in Midlem, a deed, 1756. [NRS.CC18.7.19]

THOMSON, JAMES, a burgess of Lauder, a sasine, 1779. [NRS.RS18.17.295]

THOMSON, JANET, daughter of Andrew Thomson in Kirkton of Corram, wife of Archibald Johnston a merchant in Kelso, 17.... [NRS.CC8.6.462]

THOMSON, JEAN, spouse of Mungo Thomson a burgess of Lauder, testament, 1678. C.L. [NRS]

THOMSON, JOHN, a herd in Easter Burnfoot, deeds, 1756-1759. [NRS.CC18.7.54/197]

THOMSON, JOHN, a merchant in Lauder, sasines, 1745-1779. [NRS.RS18.12.163; 13.242; 17.295]

THOMSON, MARY, from Jedburgh, guilty of infanticide, transported to the colonies in September 1773. [SM.35.557]

THOMSON, ROBERT, a wright in Bonden, a deed, 1758. [NRS.CC18.7.130]

THOMSON, THOMAS, in Lis McMurchie, parish of McKlasie, Ireland, and portioner of Earlston, Berwickshire, sasines, 12 February 1680. [NRS.RS4.181/182]

THOMSON, THOMAS, in Nether Crailing, a deed, 1758. [NRS.CC18.7.130]

THOMSON, THOMAS, in West Port of Hawick, a deed, 1756. [NRS.CC18.7.48]

The People of the Scottish Borders, 1650-1800

THOMSON, THOMAS, a carrier in Hawick, a deed, 1758. [NRS.CC18.7.143]

THOMSON, WILLIAM, a skinner in Kelso, a deed, 1757. [NRS.CC18.7.104]

THORBRAND, ALEXANDER, in Gladswood, testament, 1653. C.L. [NRS]

THORBURN, JAMES, a carrier in Coldstream, a sasine, 1762. [NRS.RS18.14.388]

THORBURN, JAMES, in Selkirk, 1783. [NRS.E326.1.210]

THORBURN, WILLIAM, portioner in Midlem, heir to his father William Thorburn, weaver and portioner in Midlem, 1769. [NRS.S/H]

TINLING, MARY, second daughter and heir to her father Thomas Tinling in Nether Ancrum, 1711. [NRS.S/H]

TOD, DAVID, a merchant in Duns, a sasine, 1708, [NRS.RS18.7.374]; testament, 1713. C.L. [NRS]

TODD, JOHN, born 1743, minister at Fogo from 1785 to 1814. [F.2.16]

TODD, JOSEPH, a merchant in Duns, a sasine, 1729. [NRS.RS18.10.343]

TOD, MARGARET, spouse of John Turnbull minister at Ayton, later in Glasgow, testament, 1792. C.L. [NRS]

TODRIG, GEORGE, a shipmaster in Eyemouth, a sasine, 1753. [NRS.RS18.13.284]

TODRIG, ROBERT, a gardener in Berwick, a sasine, 1774. [NRS.RS18.16.343]

TOFTS, MARGARET, in Fallside, testament, 1670. C.L. [NRS]

TORRIE, ARCHIBALD, minister at Newlands, and his son James Torrie, a sasine, 1700. [NRS.RS18.6.73]

TORRIE, JOSEPH, tenant in Hutton-knowhead, sasines, 1699-1707, [NRS.RS18.5.418; 7.287/289/291]; testament, 1711. C.L. [NRS]

TORRIE, ROBERT, a writer in Newbigging, Eccles, testaments, 1741/1743. C.L. [NRS]

The People of the Scottish Borders, 1650-1800

TORRIE, WILLIAM, shepherd in Corsarie, husband of Agnes Wilson born 1763, died 25 Novembe 1812. [Legerwood MI, Berwickshire]

TRENCH, ABRAHAM, in East Renton, a sasine, 1685. [NRS.RS18.4.444]

TRENCH, GEORGE, in Eyemouth, and his wife Sarah Pittie, a sasine, 1666. [NRS.RS18.1.341]

TRENT, JANET, in Greenknow, testament, 1682. C.L. [NRS]

TROTTER, ALEXANDER, a merchant in Kelso, a sasine, 1688. [NRS.RS18.5.49]

TROTTER, ALEXANDER, a maltster in Duns, testament, 1766. C.L. [NRS]

TROTTER, ANDREW, tenant in Scarlaw, testament, 1729. C.L. [NRS]

TROTTER, ARCHIBALD, born 1759, died 10 June 1771. [Ayton MI]

TROTTER, BARBARA, in Earlston, widow of Laurence Scott schoolmaster at Herriotstoun, testament, 1736. C.L. [NRS]

TROTTER, GEORGE, minister at Bunkle from 1665 to 1677, minister at Edrom from 1677. [F.2.4]

TROTTER, GEORGE, born 1728, son of John Trotter in Longnewton, died 2 July 1754. [Longnewton MI, Roxburghshire]

TROTTER, GEORGE, of Belchester, a merchant in Berwick, sasines, 1743-1773. [NRS.RS18.12.173/470; 13.85/88/99/220/230/480; 14.3; 15.82; 16.131/288]

TROTTER, JAMES, born 1719, a wright in Longnewton, died 4 November 1776. [Longnewton MI, Roxburghshire]

TROTTER, JAMES, born 1694, a smith, died 20 November 1760. [Whitsome MI]

TROTTER, JOHN, M.D. in Duns, a sasine, 1716, [NRS.RS18.9.128]; testament, 1721. C.L. [NRS]

TROTTER, JOHN, a wright in Langnewton, a deed, 1758. [NRS.CC18.7.130]

TROTTER, NINIAN, in Smailholm Mains, deeds, 1759-1760. [NRS.CC18.7.203/226/235]

The People of the Scottish Borders, 1650-1800

TROTTER, PATRICK, of Burnhouses, a sasine, 1683. [NRS.RS18.4.393]

TROTTER, PETER, born 1718, a saddler in Coldstream, died 27 June 1778, husband of Margaret Johnston. [Lennel MI, Berwickshire]

TROTTER, WILLIAM, minister at Selkirk from 1754 until his death on 4 September 1771; husband of (1) Elizabeth Mackill, (2) Janet Thomson. [F.2.195]

TROTTER, WILLIAM, a maltmaker in Duns, a sasine, 1775. [NRS.RS18.16.389]

TUCK, JOHN, in Coldingham, a sasine, 1764. [NRS.RS18.15.35]

TUDHOPE, CHARLES, a bailie and merchant in Hawick, deeds, 1756-1758. [NRS.CC18.7.43/141]

TUDHOPE, JOHN, a carrier in Hawick, a deed, 1758. [NRS.CC18.7.140]

TUDHOPE, WILLIAM, born 1690, merchant and bailie of Hawick, died 9 June 1763; his spouse Elspeth Scott, born 1686, died 11 October 1762. [Cavers MI]

TULLIE, GEORGE, a mason in Earlston, sasines, 1716-1727. [NRS.RS18.9.78; 10.24]

TUNNO, MARY, spouse of James Jack tailor in Redpath, testament, 1726. C.L. [NRS]

TURNBULL, ANDREW, in Whitehope, a deed, 1756. [NRS.CC18.7.42]

TURNBULL, ANDREW, born 1720, a plasterer in Kelso, died 14 June 1797. [Kelso MI]

TURNBULL, ELIZABETH, born 1700, spouse to Thomas Turnbull, died 13 January 1776. Cavers MI]

TURNBULL, GEORGE, a shopkeeper in Hawick, 1785. [NRS.E326.4.1]

TURNBULL, HECTOR, of Crooksfield, sasines, 1673-1706. [NRS.RS18.3.141; 7.215/218/220]

TURNBULL, JOHN, merchant in Duns, testament, 1714. C.L. [NRS]

TURNBULL, JOHN, in Minto, a deed, 1758. [NRS.CC18.7.148]

The People of the Scottish Borders, 1650-1800

TURNBULL, JOHN, a tailor in Hawick, deeds, 1757-1759. [NRS.CC18.7.87/144/197/204]

TURNBULL, JOSEPH, a shoemaker in Eyemouth, sasines, 1761-1769. [NRS.RS18.14.363; 15.241/369]

TURNBULL, RICHARD, a merchant in Eyemouth, sasines, 1751-1772. [NRS.RS18.13.126/244/457; 15.44/369; 16.163]

TURNBULL, Captain ROBERT, of Standhill, deeds, 1757. [NRS.CC18.7.65/87/214]

TURNBULL, ROBERT, tenant in Cairnsmiln, testament, 1768. C.L. [NRS]

TURNBULL, THOMAS, of Know, a deed, 1759. [NRS.CC18.7.203]

TURNBULL, THOMAS, of Minto, deeds, 1760-1761. [NRS.CC18.7.261/264/353]

TURNBULL, THOMAS, chamberlain to Sir Gilbert Elliot of Minto, deeds, 1756-1757. [NRS.CC18.7.54/95]

TURNBULL, THOMAS, a shopkeeper in Hawick, 1785. [NRS.E326.4.1]

TURNBULL, WALTER, a schoolmaster from Hawick, guilty of assault, was transported to the colonies in May 1751. [AJ.178]

TURNBULL, WILLIAM, son of William Turnbull of Makerstoun, educated at Edinburgh University, minister at Eckford, from 1666 until his death in 1677. [F.2.110]

TURNBULL, WILLIAM, bailie of the Regality of Buncle and Preston, testament, 1699. C.L. [NRS]

TURNBULL, WILLIAM, tenant in Blackadder Mains, testament, 1748. C.L. [NRS]

TURNBULL, WILLIAM, of Tofts, a bond, 1758. [NRS.CC18.7.183]

TURNBULL, WILLIAM, in Burnfoot, a deed, 1758. [NRS.CC18.7.136]

TURNBULL, WILLIAM, in Harlowmoss, a deed, 1759. [NRS.CC18.7.215]

TURNBULL, WILLIAM, in Muirhouse, a deed, 1757. [NRS.CC18.7.71]

The People of the Scottish Borders, 1650-1800

TURNBULL, WILLIAM, a glazier in Hawick, a deed, 1757. [NRS.CC18.7.95]

TURNBULL, WILLIAM, a herd in Prodds, a deed, 1758. [NRS.CC18.7.145]

TURNBULL, WILLIAM, of Rashiegrain, heir to his father Walter Turnbull of Rashiegrain, 1791. [NRS.S/H]

TURNER, ANDREW, in West Reston, testament, 1680. C.L. [NRS]

TURNER, JOHN, in Chatto, deeds, 1757-1760. [NRS.CC18.7.100/276]

TURNER, JOHN, a miller in Roxburgh Miln, a deed, 1759. [NRS.CC18.7.224]

TURNER, WILLIAM, a tailor in Caidslie, sasines, 1673-1699. [NRS.RS18.3.60/396/405; 5.419]

TWEDDIE, CHRISTIAN, spouse of Thomas Waddell in Lauder, testament, 1654. C.L. [NRS]

TWEEDIE, JANET, from Roxburghshire, guilty of infanticide, was transported to the colonies in May 1764. [SM.26.287]

UMPHERSTON, GEORGE, a weaver in Coldingham, a sasine, 1722. [NRS.RS18.9.498]

UMPHERSTON, KATHERINE, in Nisbet Pathhead, testament, 1680. C.L. [NRS]

UMPHREY, JAMES, a carpenter in Berwick, sasines, 1673-1709. [NRS.RS18.3.143; 5.278; 7.538]

URE, WILLIAM, a wright in Greenlaw, sasines, 1721-1726. [NRS.RS18.9.437/579; 10.37/57]

USHER, JOHN, in Eilden, deeds, 1758-1760. [NRS.CC18.7.172/182/260]

UTIRSTOUN, ALISON, spouse to John Tait in East Reston, testament, 1670. C.L. [NRS]

VAST, JOHN, in Halrule, deed, 1757. [NRS.CC18.7.102]

VEITCH, GEORGE, at Newmilns on Gala Water, a deed, 1757. [NRS.CC18.7.84]

The People of the Scottish Borders, 1650-1800

VEITCH, HENRY, minister at Swinton, a sasine, 1752, [NRS.RS18.13.240]; testament, 1754. C.L. [NRS]

VEITCH, JAMES, miller at Spittal Miln, a deed, 1757. [NRS.CC18.7.84]

VEITCH, JAMES, tenant in Whiteacres, Cockburnspath, testament, 1792. C.L. [NRS]

VEITCH, JOHN, a minister at Westruther, a sasine, 1691. [NRS.RS18.5.163]

VEITCH, JOHN, in Selkirk, 1783. [NRS.E326.1.210]

VEITCH, THOMAS, a gardener in Ancrum, a deed, 1757. [NRS.CC18.7.84]

VEITCH, THOMAS, gardener at Wall in the Water of Ale, a deed, 1756. [NRS.CC18.7.24]

VEITCH, WILLIAM, tenant in Redpath, testaments, 1721/1722/1742. C.L. [NRS]

VEITCH, WILLIAM, a merchant in Hawick, deeds, 1757-1758. [NRS.CC18.7.84/148]

VERTIE, ANDREW, feuar in Duns, testament, 1689. C.L. [NRS]

VIRTUE, DAVID, a tanner in Duns, sasines, 1766-1771. [NRS.RS18.15.165/275; 16.97]

VIRTUE, JOHN, a writer in Kelso, a sasine, 1780. [NRS.RS18.18.7]

VIRTUE, JOHN, born 1743, died in Coldstream on 4 May 1820, his wife Elizabeth Paterson, born 1754, died 3 March 1827. [Lennel MI]

VIRTUE, PATRICK, a shoemaker and tanner in Polwarth later in Duns, and his son Patrick Virtue, sasines, 1765-1779. [NRS.RS18.15.80/312, etc]

WADDELL, ADAM, rector of Whitsome, a sasine, 1695. [NRS.RS18.5.294]

WADDELL, ALEXANDER, in Westerraw of Greenlaw, testament, 1728. C.L. [NRS]

WADDELL, ANDREW, an apothecary in Duns, testament, 1732. C.L. [NRS]

The People of the Scottish Borders, 1650-1800

WADDELL, JOHN, a dyer and weaver in Jedburgh, deeds, 1758-1760. [NRS.CC18.7.138/296/304]

WADDELL, RICHARD, minister at Kelso, 1660-1682. [F.2.71]

WADDELL, WILLIAM, in Whitehouse, testament, 1745. C.L. [NRS]

WADDERAT, WILLIAM, in Todsmilne, testament, 1681. C.L. [NRS]

WADROPE, BARBARA, in Swintonhill, spouse to William Nisbet, testament, 1671. C.L. [NRS]

WAIT, JAMES, a herd in Crookeses, husband of Margaret Rule born 1726, died 4 September 1762. [Lennel MI, Berwickshire]

WAIT, JAMES, a shopkeeper in Kelso, 1785. [NRS.E326.4.1]

WAITT, JOHN, tenant in Wedderlie Woodheads, portioner of Greenlaw, testament, 1760. C.L. [NRS]

WALDIE, CHARLES, a merchant in Kelso, 1732. [NRS.CS228.B.2.48]

WALDIE, DAVID, a merchant in Duns, a sasine, 1773. [NRS.RS18.16.249]

WALDIE, JOHN, clerk to the Commissariat of Peebles, a tack, 1758. [NRS.CC18.7.138]

WALDIE, JOHN, a writer in Kelso, deeds, 1758-1759. [NRS.CC18.7.138/224]

WALDIE, JOHN, born 1721, in Auchencraig, died 26 May 1805, his spouse Jean Scott, born 1720, died 12 February 1759. [Chirnside MI, Berwickshire]

WALDIE, WILLIAM, an armourer and cutler in Duns, sasines, 1729-1773. [NRS.RS18.10.362; 16.249]

WALKER, JOHN, a merchant in Lauder, a sasine, 1765. [NRS.RS18.15.153]

WALKER, JOHN, a shopkeeper in Kelso, 1785. [NRS.E326.4.1]

WALKER, WILLIAM, in Upsetlington, Ladykirk, testament, 1698. C.L. [NRS]

WALKER, JOHN, in Belcher Miln, a deed, 1760. [NRS.CC18.7.275]

WALKER, WILLIAM, in Selkirk, 1783. [NRS.E326.1.210]

The People of the Scottish Borders, 1650-1800

WALKINSCHAW, ADAM, in Fogo, testament, 1679. C.L. [NRS]

WALLACE, JAMES, merchant traveller at Press, Coldingham, testament, 1712. C.L. [NRS]

WALLACE, JOHN, minister at Mertoun, testaments, 1694/1697. C.L. [NRS]

WANLESS, ARCHIBALD, born 1798 in Roxburghshire, a saddler in Charleston, South Carolina, naturalised there 11 October 1834. [NARA.M1183.1]

WARDLAW, JOHN, brother german to Patrick Wardlaw portioner of West Reston, testament, 1705. C.L. [NRS]

WARDLAW, PATRICK, of Berriehaugh, a sasine, 1705. [NRS.RS18.7.96]

WATERSTON, JOHN, a surgeon in Duns, a sasine, 1766. [NRS.RS18.15.200]

WATERSTON, WILLIAM, a wright in Duns, a sasine, 1778. [NRS.RS18.17.217]

WATHERSTON, ADAM, bailie of Langton, testament, 1764. C.L. [NRS]

WATHERSTON, ALISON, widow of William Cuthbertson portioner of Trabroun, testament, 1771. C.L. [NRS]

WATHERSTON, MUNGO, in Earnscleugh, testament, 1676. C.L. [NRS]

WATSON, ADAM, a merchant in Berwick, a sasine, 1735. [NRS.RS18.11.220]

WATSON, AGNES, in Kelso, daughter and heir of William Watson late factor to the Duke of Roxburgh, 1796. [NRS.S/H]

WATSON, ALEXANDER, town clerk of Duns, testaments, 1701/1711. C.L. [NRS]

WATSON, ANDREW, a surgeon in Kelso, sasines, 1770-1776. [NRS.RS18.16.27/411; 17.69]

WATSON, CHARLES, a maltman burgess of Lauder, testament, 1723. C.L. [NRS]

WATSON, JAMES, from Berwickshire, a merchant in Jamaica, 1769. [NRS.RS18.15.353]

WATSON, JOHN, in Over Stitchill, a Quaker, 1684. [RPCS.3/IX.681]

The People of the Scottish Borders, 1650-1800

WATSON, JOHN, a herd at Commonbrae, deeds, 1757-1758. [NRS.CC18.7.58/171]

WATSON, JOHN, a shopkeeper in Kelso, 1785. [NRS.E326.4.1]

WATSON, PETER, possibly from Selkirk, a Quaker indentured servant, to East New Jersey in 1683, settled in Perth Amboy. [Insh.247]

WATSON, ROBERT, a carter in Duns, testament, 1783. C.L. [NRS]

WATSON, WALTER, in Harwood, a deed, 1757. [NRS.CC18.7.58]

WATSON, WILLIAM, a weaver in Coldingham, sasines, 1666-1685. [NRS.RS18.1.347; 4.455]

WATSON, WILLIAM, son of James and Jane Watson in Duns, Berwickshire, a planter in Baton Rouge, West Florida, probate 1781 South Carolina

WATT, ADAM, late merchant in Kelso now in Berwick, heir to his brother John Watt in Smailholm, a feuar in Kelso, 1787. [NRS.S/H]

WATT, JAMES, in Crumstain, testament, 1676. C.L. [NRS]

WATT, PATRICK, of Rosehill, a sasine, 1692. [NRS.RS18.5.187]

WATT, WILLIAM, in Selkirk, 1783. [NRS.E326.1.210]

WATTER, ADAM, in Paxton, testaments, 1667/1669. C.L. [NRS]

WATTER, ROBERT, in Foulden, a sasine, 1681. [NRS.RS18.4.258]

WATTERS, ALISON, in Fishwick, testaments, 1676/1677. C.L. [NRS]

WAUCHOPE, ANDREW, of Edmonston, a sasine, 1759. [NRS.RS18.14.124]

WAUCHOPE, JAMES, of Comiston, late tenant in Sligh's houses, testament, 1757. C.L. [NRS]

WAUGH, or FISHER, CHRISTIAN, in Jedburgh, a deed, 1756. [NRS.CC18.7.49]

WAUGH, JAMES, in Ligertwood, a sasine, 1715. [NRS.RS18.9.26]

WAUGH, PATRICK, in Boncle, testament, 1655. C.L. [NRS]

The People of the Scottish Borders, 1650-1800

WAUGH, ROBERT, minister at Hutton, testament, 1756. C.L. [NRS]

WAUGH, THOMAS, a writer in Jedburgh, deeds, 1756-1761. [NRS.CC18.7.38/49/107/116/124/173/182/206/221/234/339]

WAUGH, THOMAS, from Jedburgh, a factor and a surgeon, settled in New York before 1778. [NRS.GD5]

WAUGH, Commissary, in Selkirk, 1783. [NRS.E326.1.210]

WEATHERBY, THOMAS, in Paxton, a sasine, 1779. [NRS.RS18.17.378]

WEATHERHEAD, ALEXANDER, a baker in Coldstream, a sasine, 1775. [NRS.RS18.16.428]

WEATHERHEAD, ROBERT, a butcher and innkeeper in Coldstream, sasines, 1750. [NRS.RS18.13.72/79]

WEATHERHEAD, THOMAS, shopkeeper in Coldstream, 1785.[NRS.E326.4.1]

WEDDERBURN, ISOBEL, spouse to William Cleghorn, testament, 1675. C.L. [NRS]

WEDDERBURN, JAMES, in Nickilside of Coldingham, testament, 1670. C.L. [NRS]

WEDDERBURN, JAMES, a maltman in Coldingham, a sasine, 1695. [NRS.RS18.5.293]

WEDDERBURN, JOHN, a mason in Coldingham, a sasine, 1754. [NRS.RS18.13.400]

WEDDERLY, JAMES, tenant in Foulden Hill, testament, 1776. C.L. [NRS]

WEDDERSTON, JOHN, son of John Wedderston in Galashiels, a surgeon who settled in Kingston, Jamaica, before 1773. [NRS.CS.GMB.7.73]

WEIGHT, JOHN, in Mellerstaines, testament, 1770. C.L. [NRS]

WEIR, AGNES, a vintner in Duns, testament, 1785. C.L. [NRS]

WEIR, GEORGE, in Heughhead, sasines, 1767-1774. [NRS.RS18.15.243/385/387; 16.342]

The People of the Scottish Borders, 1650-1800

WEIR, JOHN, former merchant in Edinburgh, residing in Duns, testament, 1729. C.L. [NRS]

WEIR, JOHN, born 1730, senior schoolmaster, died 30 December 1802. [Kelso MI]

WEIR, PATRICK, a wright in Damside, a deed, 1760. [NRS.CC18.7.291]

WELSH, ADAM, in Burnfoot, deeds, 1757. [NRS.CC18.7.110/123/124]

WELSH, JAMES, a chapman in Horndean, testament, 1671. C.L. [NRS]

WELSH, MATTHEW, grandson of Hohn Howison, a merchant in Duns, a sasine, 1700. [NRS.RS18.6.182]

WESTGARTH, JOHN, a Lieutenant of the 99th Regiment of Foot, testament, 1770. C.L. [NRS]

WHALE, ANDREW, a tailor in London, heir to his immediate younger brother Lancelot Whale, Rector of Kelso Grammar School, 1793, and to his nephew Robert Whale or Wales, only son of the said Lancelot. [NRS.S/H]

WHILLAS, GEORGE, a notary in Duns, son of Robert Whillas a notary there, sasines, 1708-1723. [NRS.RS18.7.382; 9.598]

WHILLAS, ROBERT, a writer in Duns, testament, 1732. C.L. [NRS]

WHILLAS, THOMAS, a horse-cooper in Duns, sasines, 1745-1746. [NRS.RS18.12.176/179/225]

WHILLAS, WILLIAM, in Coldstream, son of William Whillas minister at Lessingham, testament, 1704. C.L. [NRS]

WHILLIE, ROBERT, a labourer in Coldstream, and his spouse Agnes Dickson, a sasine, 1761. [NRS.RS18.14.377]

WHITE, DAVID, born 1761, schoolmaster at Duns for 36 years, died 18 August 1822, his spouse Mary Johnston, born 1743, died 17 March 1798, their son William White, born 1780, died in Virginia on 18 October 1814. [Duns MI]

WHITE, GEORGE, tenant in Fogo Nook, testament, 1753. C.L. [NRS]

The People of the Scottish Borders, 1650-1800

WHITE, JOHN, a gardener in Duns, a sasine, 1765. [NRS.RS18.15.128]

WHYTE, PATRICK, tenant in Longnewton, father of John White born 1723, died 1736, and Andrew Whyte, born 1728, died 1742. [Longnewton MI]

WHITE, ROBERT, a cabinetmaker in Coldstream, a sasine, 1777. [NRS.RS18.17.113]

WHITE, THOMAS, in Nisbet, testament, 1787. C.L. [NRS]

WHITE, WILLIAM, from Roxburghshire, a thief who was transported to the colonies in September 1753. [SM.15.468][AJ.298]

WHITHEAD, JANET, in Chapelhill of Cockburnspath, testament, 1684. C.L. [NRS]

WHITHEAD, PATRICK, in Eyemouth, a sasine, 1755. [NRS.RS18.13.419]

WHITELAW, JOHN, a candlemaker in Duns, a sasine, 1771. [NRS.RS18.16.107]

WHITLAW, ROBERT, a maltster in Melrose, a deed, 1756. [NRS.CC18.7.48]

WHITLIE, JAMES, a smith in Ayton, and his son Patrick Whitlie, sasines, 1770-1776. [NRS.RS18.15.425; 17.71/73]

WHITLIE, JAMES, born 1722, a smith in Ayton, died 4 March 1773. His spouse Magdalene Gray born 1731, died 11 July 1800, son John born 1751, died 9 September 1772. [Ayton MI, Berwickshire]

WHITLIE, JAMES, born 1757, feuar in Ayton, died 25 July 1845, his wife Isabel Clark, born 1766, died 6 December 1837, their son John Whitlie born 1800, died in South Trenton, New Jersey, 30 April 1847. [Ayton MI, Berwickshire]

WHITLIE, WILLIAM, in Grocdykes, testament, 1679. C.L. [NRS]

WHITELOCK, RICHARD, born 1743, a flesher in Kelso, died 27 January 1794. [Kelso MI]

WHITSON, JOHN, schoolmaster in Ayton, sasines, 1715-1729. [NRS.RS18.8.594/596; 9.35]

WIGHT, ALEXANDER, in Ayton, testament, 1700. C.L. [NRS]

WIGHT, DAVID, a weaver in Ayton, sasine, 1756. [NRS.RS18.13.509]

The People of the Scottish Borders, 1650-1800

WIGHT, JOHN, a mason in Longformacus, a sasine, 1773. [NRS.RS18.16.299]

WIGHT, ROBERT, a flesher in Ayton, testament, 1736. C.L. [NRS]

WIGHT, WILLIAM, born 1750, died 8 April 1816, his daughter Frances, born 1791, died 23 January 1796. [Mindrum MI]

WIGHTMAN, JAMES, a carrier in Coldstream, sasines, 1768. [NRS.RS18.15.324/325]

WIGHTMAN, THOMAS, tenant in Whiterig, testament, 1763. C.L. [NRS]

WIGTON, WILLIAM, in Liston Milne, testament, 1655. C.L. [NRS]

WIGTON, WILLIAM, born 1776, a paper-maker at Broomhouse Paper Mill, died 13 July 1816. [Duns MI]

WILD, JOHN, a notary in Coldingham, a sasine, 1668. [NRS.RS18.2.72]

WILD, PATRICK, feuar in Coldstream, a sasine, 1754. [NRS.RS18.13.377]

WILKIE, JAMES, of Foulden, chamberlain to Lord Ross, sasines, 1696-1733, [NRS.RS18.5.323, etc]; testaments, 1733/1737. C.L. [NRS]

WILKIE, ROBERT, a herd at Houspaslay, a deed, 1760. [NRS.CC18.7.278]

WILKIE, THOMAS, minister at Galashiels 1665-1672. [F.2.177]

WILKIE, THOMAS, a merchant in Hawick, a deed, 1758. [NRS.CC18.7.171]

WILKIE, THOMAS, a smith in Maxton, a deed, 1759. [NRS.CC18.7.213]

WILKIE, ZACHARIAH, minister at Ellem, sasine, 1677, [NRS.RS18.4.56]; testament, 1684. C.L. [NRS]

WILKIESON, THOMAS, a wright in Leithfield, sasines, 1744-1774. [NRS.RS18.12.105; 14.128; 16.311]

WILKIESON, THOMAS, of Chesterhall, a deed, 1760. [NRS.CC18.7.247]

WILKISON, ALEXANDER, burgess of Lauder, testament, 1680. C.L. [NRS]

WILLIAMS, WILLIAM, a wright at Spittle of Rule, a deed, 1760. [NRS.CC18.7.304]

WILLIAMSON, CHARLES, a shopkeeper in Kelso, 1785. [NRS.E326.4.1]

WILLIAMSON, JAMES, a mason in Duns, a sasine, 1761. [NRS.RS18.14.321]

WILLIAMSON, JOHN, a burgess of Peebles, his wife Bessie Robertson, their second son William and their third son John, in Bonnington, Peebles, 1654. [RGS.X.332]

WILLIAMSON, JOHN, formerly a merchant in Edinburgh, residing in Duns, testament, 1707. C.L. [NRS]

WILLIAMSON, PAUL, servant to James the Earl of Home, sasines, 1682/1683. [NRS.RS18.4.330/377]

WILSON, ALEXANDER, a baxter in Home, a sasine, 1733. [NRS.RS18.11.105]

WILSON, ANDREW, died 11 September 1812, his wife Elizabeth Aitken, died 12 June 1819. [Kelso Episcopal MI]

WILSON, ANNE, from Roxburghshire, a thief and pickpocket, spouse of David Douglas, was transported to the colonies in September 1766. [AJ.979]

WILSON, CHARLES, a shoemaker in Eyemouth, sasines, 1753-1756. [NRS.RS18.13.325/510]

WILSON, DAVID, in Greenlaw of Foulden, sasines, 1746-1750. [NRS.RS18.12.209; 13.68]

WILSON, GEORGE, schoolmaster of Duns, testament, 1781. C.L. [NRS]

WILSON, JAMES, in Millstead, a deed, 1761. [NRS.CC18.7.341]

WILSON, JOHN, a mason in Eyemouth, testament, 1752. C.L. [NRS]

WILSON, JOHN, a weaver in Hawick, a deed, 1758. [NRS.CC18.7.136]

WILSON, MATTHEW, in Coldingham, a sasine, 1666. [NRS.RS18.1.331]

WILSON, MICHAEL, and his spouse Janet Clerk in Paxton, testament, 1677. C.L. [NRS]

WILSON, ROBERT, a smith in Blackadder, testament, 1676. C.L. [NRS]

The People of the Scottish Borders, 1650-1800

WILSON, ROBERT, in Mains, a deed, 1757. [NRS.CC18.7.101]

WILSON, ROBERT, in Maisondiew, a deed, 1758. [NRS.CC18.7.165]

WILSON, THOMAS, schoolmaster in Halnash, a deed, 1758. [NRS.CC18.7.179]

WILSON, THOMAS, an innkeeper in Kelso, Roxburghshire, 1768-1774. [NRS.CS96.3835]

WILSON, WALTER, a shopkeeper in Hawick, 1785. [NRS.E326.4.1]

WILSON, WILLIAM, a writer in Hawick, a deed, 1757. [NRS.CC18.7.124]

WILSON, WILLIAM, born 1721, eldest son of James Wilson, died 10 June 1780. [Earlston MI, Berwickshire]

WILSON, WILLIAM, born 1738, a barber and feuar in Duns, died 9 March 1800, his spouse Isobel Boog, born 1739, died 15 December 1778. [Duns MI.]

WILSON, Mrs, a shopkeeper in Kelso, 1785. [NRS.E326.4.1]

WINCHESTER, JAMES, minister at Jedburgh from 1734 until his death on 18 September 1755, husband of Mary Dunbar, parents of Christian, James, William, Margaret, and John. [F.2.127]

WINRAM, GEORGE, of Eyemouth, sasines, 1689-1713. [NRS.RS18.5.102, etc]

WINRAM, JAMES, of Oxendean, sheriff-clerk of Berwick, sasines, 1745-1756, [NRS.RS18.12.146/227; 13.342/514/562]; testament, 1756. C.L. [NRS]

WINTER, JANET, spouse to Robert Dalgleish in Wadderlie, testament, 1664. C.L. [NRS]

WINTER, PETER, born 1705, joiner to the Earls of Marchmont, died 17 December 1802, husband of Alison Jaffery, born 1712, died 15 March 1790. [Polwarth MI, Berwickshire]

WINTER, WILLIAM, born 1789, son of William Winter, of the 91st Regiment, died at Fort Augusta, Jamaica, on 23 December 1825. [Polwarth MI, Berwickshire]

WINTROPE, JAMES, in Hawick, a bond, 1775. [NRS.RD4.207.589]

The People of the Scottish Borders, 1650-1800

WINTROPE, THOMAS, a writer in Hawick, a deed, 1757. [NRS.CC18.7.105]

WISHART, Colonel GEORGE, of Cliftonhall, sasines, 1764. [NRS.RS18.15.9/12/14/18]

WODERLIE, JOHN, a webster in Coldingham, testament, 1653. C.L. [NRS]

WOOD, ADAM, servant to Alexander Home of Manderston, testament, 1752. C.L. [NRS]

WOOD, JAMES, a weaver in Muirhead, testament, 1724. C.L. [NRS]

WOOD, JAMES, a surgeon in Berwick, a sasine, 1758. [NRS.RS18.13.538]

WOOD, JOHN, a burgess of Lauder, a sasine, 1697. [NRS.RS18.5.345]

WOOD, THOMAS, a bailie of Lauder, a sasine, 1725. [NRS.RS18.10.46]

WOOD, THOMAS, a herd in Borthwick, testament, 1764. C.L. [NRS]

WOOD, WILLIAM, a tenant in East Gordon, testament, 1725. C.L. [NRS]

WORTHINGTON, HANNAH, spouse of Captain John Pringle a merchant in Eyemouth, a sasine, 1754. [NRS.RS18.13.398]

WRIGHT, BESSY, in Maxwellheugh, died 1689, a Quaker. [NRS.SQR.K17]

WRIGHT, JOHN, a merchant in Duns, testament, 1655. C.L. [NRS]

WRIGHT, PATRICK, son of John Wright, a merchant in Duns, a sasine, 1697. [NRS.RS18.5.342]

WRIGHT, WILLIAM, a farmer in Greengelt, testament, 1699. C.L. [NRS]

WYLD, JOHN, feuar of Coldingham, testaments, 1695/1697/1699. C.L. [NRS]

WYLLIE, PATRICK, servant to James the Earl of Home, a sasine, 1663. [NRS.RS18.1.78]

WYLLIE, ROBERT, minister at Ashkirk, Selkirkshire, from 1691 to 1692. [F.2.169]

YEAMAN, JOHN, a farmer from Edington, Berwickshire, a Covenanter who was transported from Leith aboard the St Michael of Scarborough bound for the West Indies on 12 December 1678. [RPCS.6.76]

The People of the Scottish Borders, 1650-1800

YEAMAN, MARGARET, relict of John Dallas bailie of Duns, testaments, 1742/1743/1749. C.L. [NRS]

YEAMAN, THOMAS, a gardener in Chalkielaw, a sasine, 1771. [NRS.RS18.16.103]

YEAMAN, WILLIAM, in Edington Mains, testament, 1672. C.L. [NRS]

YEAMAN, WILLIAM, a farmer from Edington, Berwickshire, a Covenanter who was transported from Leith aboard the St Michael of Scarborough bound for the West Indies on 12 December 1678. [RPCS.6.76]

YEATES, BENJAMIN, born 1702 in Berwick, emigrated via London on 9 April 1720 bound for Virginia. [CLRO/AIA]

YELLOWLEES, THOMAS, in Whitsome, sasines, 1658-1688. [NRS.RS18.4.5/39/100; 5.58]

YELLOWLEES, THOMAS, in Mellerstaines, testaments, 1669/1670. C.L. [NRS]

YEOMAN, JOHN, a gardener in Duns, died 11 October 1791. [Duns MI]

YOLE, JAMES, tenant of Shannabent, died 1 April 1777, husband of Elizabeth Brown. [Abbey St Bathans, MI, Berwickshire]

YORSTOUN, JANET, from Roxburghshire, a gypsy who was transported from Glasgow on 1 January 1715 bound for Virginia. [GR.530]

YORSTOUN, MARY, from Roxburghshire, a thief and vagabond who was transported to the colonies in May 1732. [NRS.JC.12.4]

YOUNG, ALEXANDER, a surgeon apothecary in Selkirk, sasines, 1714-1744. [NRS.RS18.8.525; 10.497; 12.111]

YOUNG, ANDREW, a tailor in Eyemouth, sasines, 1661. [NRS.RS18.4.167/177]

YOUNG, GEORGE, from Teviotdale, a Covenanter who was transported from Leith in August 1685 bound for Jamaica, landed at Port Royal in November 1685. [RPCS.II.329][LJ.17]

YOUNG, GEORGE, only son of John Young a surgeon apothecary in Coldstream and his first wife Jane Mason, testament, 1742. C.L. [NRS]

The People of the Scottish Borders, 1650-1800

YOUNG, GEORGE, a sailor in Eyemouth, a sasine, 1755. [NRS.RS18.13.482]

YOUNG, JAMES, a farmer from Home, Berwickshire, a fireraiser who was transported to the colonies in October 1748. [SM.10.499]

YOUNG, JEANY, a merchant in Jedburgh, a deed, 1756. [NRS.CC18.7.37]

YOUNG, JOHN, a soldier from Roxburghshire, a thief who was transported, with his wife Margaret Young, to the colonies in October 1749. [SM.II.509]

YOUNG, JOHN, a surgeon apothecary in Coldstream, testaments, 1749/1760. C.L. [NRS]

YOUNG, JOHN, in Stow, a deed, 1769. [NRS.RD4.218.740]

YOUNG, MARK, from Barnhills, Roxburghshire, a Covenanter who was transported to the colonies in October 1684. [RPCS.9.449]

YOUNG, RALPH, in Cornhill Boathouse, sasines, 1749-1765. [NRS.RS18.12.460; 15.95/97/100]

YOUNG, WILLIAM, from Berwickshire, in Kingston, Jamaica, sasines, 1773/1776. [NRS.RS18.16.222/451]

YOUNG, WILLIAM, born 1757, a merchant in Kelso, died 14 January 1799. [Kelso MI]

YOUNGER, CHRISTIAN, in Easter Prentonen, testament, 1676. C.L. [NRS]

YOUNGER, JOHN, a tailor in Fishwick, 1663. [NRS.RS18.1.96]

YOUNGHUSBAND, THOMAS, tenant in Longnewton, died June 1799, his spouse Isabella Murray, born 1735, died 1809, parents of Isabella and Agnes. [Longnewton MI, Roxburghshire]

YUILL, HENRY, a millwright in Ayton, a sasine, 1778. [NRS.RS18.17.185]

YUILL, PATRICK, in Mellerstaines, testament, 1665. C.L. [NRS]

YUILL, THOMAS, maltman in Mellerstaines, testament, 1687. C.L. [NRS]

www.ingramcontent.com/pod-product-compliance
Lightning Source LLC
Chambersburg PA
CBHW072142160426
43197CB00012B/2216